BLOWN AWAY

A year through the lens of **The Tornado Hunter** | **Greg Johnson**

The
TORNADOHUNTER

indie ink
PUBLISHING

Published by
Indie Ink Publishing
610 Rusholme Road
Saskatoon, SK, Canada S7L 0G7
T 306.664.2723

Printed in Canada by
Friesens Book Division

First edition: April, 2012

ISBN 978-0-9878105-1-9

Library and Archives Canada Cataloguing in Publication
Johnson, Greg, 1970
Blown away : a year through the lens of the tornado hunter / Greg Johnson.
Includes index.

ISBN 978-0-9878105-1-9

1. Tornadoes–United States–Pictorial works.
2. Storms–United States–Pictorial works. I. Title.

QC955.5.U6J63 2012   779'.9551553092   C2011-908345-0

Book Design: Serge Bourgault (sergebourgault.com)
Editor: Tammy Robert

CHASER MAP

- ● TORNADO ALLEY
- ● PROVINCES & STATES CHASED IN

SASKATCHEWAN

MANITOBA

MONTANA

NORTH DAKOTA

SOUTH DAKOTA

WYOMING

ILLINOIS

NEBRASKA

COLORADO

KANSAS

MISSOURI

OKLAHOMA

ARKANSAS

MISSISSIPI

TEXAS

TABLE OF CONTENTS

To *Olivia*…Maintain your adventurous spirit and remember to forge your own path.
I know you will be successful in anything you want to do.

To *Cooper*…You are a strong and respectful boy. No father could be as proud
of their son as I am of you. Never give up.

To *Gabby*…You are the source of laughter in our home. You always know that
my favorite thing in the world is hearing you sing.

Wanita, you are patient, composed, driven, poised, funny, understanding and
supportive. It really is an incredible adventure that we are on.
I can't wait to write the next chapter.

———————————————

*This book is also dedicated to the memory of Andy Gabrielson, storm chasing's superstar who
was killed in a car accident in February, 2012. Andy was a tremendous person who left
a positive impression on everyone he met. He set the 'gold standard' for storm chasers and
was widely recognized as being the best in the business. I learned a great deal from Andy
and for that, I thank him.*

ACKNOWLEDGEMENTS
BLOWN AWAY

First and foremost I must give a huge hug and thank you to my family. My beautiful wife Wanita and our children, Olivia, Cooper and Gabby give me up for weeks at a time to pursue my dream, and do it with love and pride, for which I remain forever grateful. I love you. Go Team Tornado Johnson!

I want to thank my parents, Pat and Doug Johnson, for all of their help, advice and support over the years. I am sure that if I started today, it would take an eternity to repay them all they have given me.

When a photographer or writer dreams of their first book, it usually ends there. I had the good fortune of meeting Suzanne and Jeff from Indie Ink who immediately saw value in this project and drew me into the secret world of book publishing. Getting this first book finished is a huge accomplishment and it could not have happened without these amazing people.

People come and go from our lives but sometimes you meet someone that you just know is going to play a huge role in your personal storyline. My publicist and the editor of this book, Tammy Robert, came into my crazy life in 2011 and has played such a big role ever since. I am glad she is on my team.

Although the photos and stories on these pages are my personal mosaic, this book in its entirety is an artistic masterpiece that required a lot of work and a lot of late nights. Serge Bourgault designed it and I cannot comprehend how much time and energy he poured into it. Thank you, Serge.

Big thanks to my friends Dallas, Jaclyn, Martin, Vanessa, Angie, Nick, Notanee and Preston. They have spent a ton of time talking, learning and experiencing storms and photography with me—and way too much time sitting in my truck.

I also want to recognize our drivers—the pilots on these mad adventures. I am always looking for drivers and this past year had some great ones: Derek Bosche, Justin Locke, Howard Robinson, Rich Brandvold and David Sampson.

And finally, I want to thank you, for joining me on this journey: by reading this book, following me on Twitter, @canadogreg, becoming a Facebook fan, or stopping by my website. I hope you'll stay with me as I continue down this awe-inspiring, terrifying, humbling and magnificent road.

Greg Johnson

FOREWORD
GEORGE KOUROUNIS

The 2011 tornado season in the United States was record breaking. Unfortunately, not for its lack of tornadoes, but rather for the extreme number of these twisting menaces that touched down in America's heartland and their seeming preponderance for striking urban centers rather than open farmland.

Whenever a tornado touches down, there's usually a small group of us dedicated weather watchers following close by in the shadow of the tornado with our cameras at the ready, spending weeks at a time on the road with the aim of capturing that perfect photo of Nature's most powerful winds. We are storm chasers, and we live like nomads each spring, going wherever the wind takes us. Canadian photographer and tornado hunter Greg Johnson expertly captures the essence of what it's like to be on the road, in hot pursuit of these monster storms. *Blown Away: A year through the lens of The Tornado Hunter* is his chronicle of what became a tornado season that many will never forget.

From the adrenaline high of spotting a photogenic tornado crossing an open field, to the horror and disbelief of the sunrise view the day after a tornado ravaged the city of Joplin, Missouri, Greg captures each moment with his camera, freezing the emotion of that instant forever, with stunning and sometimes sobering results.

It's not uncommon for storm chasers to meet up in an obscure corner of "Tornado Alley," whether it's a gas station in Ogallala, Nebraska or a restaurant parking lot in Norman, Oklahoma. We're all targeting the same areas, making our forecasts and reading the sky with the same thing in mind: Finding that elusive spot where we think a tornado is most likely to touch down. These convergences of storm chasers are more than a confirmation of our forecasts, they are an important social element in the brotherhood of storm chasing. This is exactly how Greg and I first met, in a hotel parking lot.

Greg's rare combination of skills has allowed him to get into places where most sane people are evacuating from, and do it in a safe manner. He embraces each day pursuing his passion for extreme weather events. These weather events only become disasters when they impact populated areas. A tornado that churns away across an open field remains a spectacle of nature but never makes that transition to a natural disaster, and even though we storm chasers want to see tornadoes, we never wish for them to impact communities. If they do, however, we're there to document the event and send in our weather observations to help issue warnings to other communities that might be unfortunate enough to find themselves in the path.

Greg's photographs of the aftermath of the devastating Joplin EF-5 tornado are particularly striking. I remember that storm very well. It was my birthday, and I was looking forward to a good chase. It was the very first day of a new tour that I was helping to guide, and everybody was in a great mood. The storm that eventually produced the Joplin tornado started off looking ragged and disorganized. I never expected it to amount to much more than some gusty winds, torrential rain and perhaps some hail for the people of Joplin.

That was the case—until it reached the edge of town.

Almost like flicking a switch, the storm took on a textbook-perfect shape on our radar screens, and the reports of a large, damaging tornado started to come in over the radio. My stomach sank, and at that moment I knew that there were people struggling for their lives. As we got closer to where the tornado was, it became clear that we would probably never see it, the circulation had become completely wrapped in rain which makes this type of storm so much more dangerous. The tornado could barrel over the top of you and you'd never even see it coming until the last second.

I paced my driving to keep a safe distance back. Debris started falling out of the sky. We encountered at least a dozen vehicles flipped over on their sides, many of which were 18-wheelers with full loads. The tornado had just crossed the highway ahead of us, missing us by no more than a few minutes.

We immediately became first responders, running in the pouring rain from truck to truck, checking on the condition of the drivers inside. One had a serious head wound so we took him to the local hospital, not knowing at the time that it had taken a direct hit from the tornado and was heavily damaged.

As I was getting out of town, Greg was blasting north to make it to the scene. The next morning, he was capturing the amazing images seen in these pages as rescue crews were searching through the rubble.

I hope you enjoy Greg's photography as much as I do. His blend of artistic and journalistic styles punctuates his storytelling, bringing the reader along for the ride...and what a ride it is!

George Kourounis

George Kourounis
Storm Chaser & Adventurer
Host of the *Angry Planet* TV series

To me, Blown Away is a metaphor on three levels:

2011 changed my life. I sold the business I had for 10 years with the goal of pursuing storm chasing as a career—only the second individual in Canada to do so. I have been Blown Away by the experience, and the fact that I have been able to celebrate so much personal and professional success.

Being thrust into the unimaginable scene at Joplin, Missouri in May, 2011 was a life changer. The experience challenged me to face my own mortality. I was Blown Away at the level of devastation, the power of mother nature and the ability of people to survive and move on.

Perhaps it's a function of getting older, or maybe I have watched too many Steve Jobs speeches but in 2011 I was Blown Away by the realization of my purpose in life—passing on an amazing legacy to my children.

INTRODUCTION
BLOWN AWAY

In 1990 my grandfather packed up his bicycle, boarded a cargo ship at the port of Vancouver and began an adventure that would take him to New Zealand, where at times he biked close to 60 miles a day. He helped one local farmer repair two hundred vegetable crates. He slept in small town motels along the way, exploring caves and hiking trails during the day.

He was 85 years old and this was not his first escapade. He had once been the guest of the University of Pittsburgh on an amazing trip that took him around the world in four months. He was a 'wise old owl' on the Semester-at-Sea program. Again, both experiences he had in his 80s.

My parents, Pat and Doug, share this philosophy. They are in their late 60s now and still travel the globe in search of the most awe-inspiring places on the planet. In 2011 alone they travelled to Peru, Ireland, Newfoundland, Portugal, Australia and Italy. What an incredible legacy they are passing on to me.

In his best-selling book *Outliers*, Malcolm Gladwell discusses the 10,000 hour rule: if you want to truly become successful and world class at anything you need to get your 10,000 hours of practice in. Thanks to circumstance, timing, the economy and a whole host of other factors, I got my 10,000 hours of photography in pretty early.

I've had the opportunity to work with some great photographers over the past 15 years and going back as far as high school I learned from the best. Brad Borbridge was the guy who first introduced me to the world of Single Lens Reflex (SLR) photography and processing my own black and white film in the basement. I guess that was a watershed moment, because I have been a photographer since receiving that first lesson from him.

Yes, it was an interesting journey between where I began–the world of sports and commercial photography–and the world of storm chasing and extreme photography. An interesting journey, but not a difficult one.

Canadians are obsessed with weather and I am no exception. Clouds, storms and ultimately tornadoes make beautiful photography subjects. Plus, I won't lie: I'm an adrenaline junkie, so storm chasing suits me nicely.

I decided to write this book after the 2011 chase season. I did not shoot a single photo in the book thinking that they would ever be published. The simple fact was that the 2011 storm season was off-the-charts epic and I knew that something needed to be done with these images.

Today I am considered a severe weather expert, a tag I am humbly willing to embrace. I have learned so much about weather forecasting, understanding radar images and storm structure as I have learned how to chase. I now bookmark weather websites, read weather blogs and follow weather personalities.

In fact, I am now a full-fledged weather nerd.

The storm chase community has been very good to me. I have had the opportunity to meet, travel and share information with many of the elite within the fraternity, a relatively small group of individuals that give up their weekends, vacation time or even their careers to pursue chasing. Chasers are either meteorologists, photographers/videographers or journalists–but at heart, we are all thrill seekers.

Something I've come to understand very clearly is that this whole storm chasing thing is a lot harder than it looks. Intercepting a tornado is a very rare experience, even for those of us that are hunting them using excellent weather forecasting from the professionals, in-vehicle technology and the proliferation of cell-based web access. There were many times this season alone that saw our team positioned under a rotating storm, with a good visual, a tornado warning in effect and the storm simply didn't hold up its end of the bargain.

The good news for me is that as a photographer I am rarely at a loss for something to shoot. Severe weather doesn't always produce a tornado but always produces spectacular sights to photograph.

One aspect of storm chasing that I really enjoy is the people; I had the pleasure of chasing with a wide variety of them this season. I met the Columbia, Missouri "boys" Chris Thompson, Ian Young and Cody Robertson. I also met my Iowa connection, Robert Keller and my Illinois connection, John Paul Goelz. I forged ties with an amazing group of chasers from North Carolina: Team Red–Brandon, Ryan, Armando and Allyce. I met stalwarts of the business like David Drummond, Daniel Shaw and Scott McPartland under the dark black clouds of Tornado Alley.

I chased with great local heroes as well: Dallas Hicks, Jaclyn Whittal, Notanee Bourassa, Nick Schenher, Martin Weaver, Vanessa Neufeld, Angie Wagar, Jess Leverington, David Sampson, Derek Bosche and Preston Kanak. I had the great pleasure of building a friendship with George Kourounis of *Angry Planet* fame and Mark Robinson from *The Weather Network*.

These great people, as well as the thousands of weather junkies that I connected with on Twitter and Facebook helped make this adventure a reality for me.

Throughout the book I have added Chaser Code. These linguistic snippets will hopefully draw you even deeper into the world of storm chasing–into my world. You will learn some of the slang and perhaps also get a better understanding of how chasing is accomplished.

I have also added technical information about each photo–the three critical components of photography: Aperture, Shutter Speed & ISO. These have been included for the benefit of the photography crowd, to give them a glimpse into how each photo was taken.

Some chapters are short, some are long, because some chases are a day or two and some last for weeks. Chapters are chronological and will take you through one entire chase season, from its beginning in Missouri in mid-April, to its last Canadian lightning strike north of the border in August. The images and stories criss-cross Tornado Alley, taking you along for the ride as I experienced the most prolific storm season in decades.

Before you embark on this journey with me, I want to begin by throwing down a challenge.

Steve Jobs said "Your time is limited, so don't waste it living someone else's life."

I subscribe wholeheartedly to this notion and want to challenge you to find your own adventure, create your own stories and ensure that you are leaving a valuable legacy for your own children. Who knows, maybe someday I will meet you along the road, somewhere in Tornado Alley.

"A dramatic lowering out of the base of the storm made it clear that a tornado was imminent, but as we photographed the scene, the most intense lightning strike imaginable forced us back into the truck."

CHAPTER 1
INITIATION

ILLINOIS
MISSOURI
TEXAS
ARKANSAS

f2.8
1/80
ISO 1600

The "Green-Sky Supercell"
spawned several funnels and
at least two tornadoes.

CHAPTER 1
INITIATION

ILLINOIS
MISSOURI
TEXAS
ARKANSAS

◉ **REGINA** SK

◉ **BISMARK** ND

◉ **ST. LOUIS** MO
○ LITCHFIELD IL

○ COLUMBIA MO

○ SPRINGFIELD MO

○ MCALESTER OK

○ SHERMAN TX

○ BAIRD TX

○ TEXARKANA TX

○ ROLLA MO

◉ LITTLE ROCK AR

○ COAHOMA MI

○ HELENA AR

○ BEEBE AR

○ VELONIA AR

◉ REGINA SK

APRIL 17, 2011
DAY 1:

My list of names had been exhausted trying to find someone to join me on the trip of a lifetime.

It should have been easy—who wouldn't want to go on a storm chase? The upcoming weeks forecasted wave after wave of severe weather in the American South. Tornadoes were a real possibility.

Despite my best efforts, on April 17, 2011, I began my first journey alone. The Tornado Truck was fuelled and loaded: passport, phone, wallet, camera, video camera, tripod, shorts, t-shirts, hiking boots, hat and sunglasses. Sporting a new look (in January I began growing my hair...it was longer than ever) and a new outlook on life, I headed for the border.

Guards asked the regular questions: Where are you going? For how long? Where are you staying? Is the purpose of your trip business or pleasure? I guess I missed the sign that said "Long haired freaky people need not apply," because the next hour and a half were spent trapped inside a tiny room, while three exuberant guards grilled me with questions and dismantled my truck.

Back on the road two hours later, I was behind schedule but none the worse for wear.

The 2011 chase season had officially begun.

APRIL 19 - 23, 2011
DAY 2 - 6:

The next morning, Bismarck, North Dakota was covered in a blanket of thick heavy snow. With well over 745 miles ahead, my butt would be put to the test.

Next stop…Columbia, Missouri.

The first thing I did was check the forecast. It did not disappoint. Both the models and the forecasters were saying the same thing–rampant tornado potential. In the right place at the right time, the task now was to find a twister. Given the complicated network of roads and challenging Missouri terrain, that would be no easy feat. Map in hand and course plotted, I repacked my truck and hit the road.

Target: St. Louis, Missouri.

Hitting the metro area, the radar indicated that a series of storms was developing to the southwest. It was time to get some food, fuel, and to formulate a plan of attack. The van in front of me displayed the **SKYWARN®** logo. It made sense to follow, introduce myself and get the lay of the land from a local chaser.

At the next exit I met first-time chasers Ian, Cody and Chris, along with another group from Illinois and Iowa. Together we formulated a plan: head east from St. Louis and wait for storms to cross the Mississippi River, where we could intercept them on more favorable terrain. At the first rest stop outside St. Louis we pulled over to check the radar–a tornado warning had just been issued: the chase was on. Heading west, then north, we positioned ourselves for interception.

The three vehicles in our chase convoy stopped dead as a perfect **wall cloud** descended from the base of the storm in front of us. As we watched, this strong rotation passed directly overhead, producing a beautiful funnel which quickly dissipated, but given the downed power poles everywhere, we knew we were in the right area.

Following the **mesocyclone,** our convoy moved east with the storm. As we watched we got word from a fellow chaser that prior to this storm crossing into Illinois, it had produced a couple of tornadoes near Bowling Green, Missouri.

Intensity in the vehicle was peaking with only a half hour of daylight left. It was Day 1 of the 2011 chase season and I felt great about my ability to get to the right spot at the right time...but we had yet to see a tornado. It was all up to the storm, and 15 minutes later even an untrained storm watcher could see that it was finished. Radar, which is about five minutes behind real time, told the same story. We had been close, but it wasn't going to happen.

Pictured left to right, Ian Young, Cody Robertson, John Paul Goelz, Chris Thompson and Robert Keller...fellow chasers that I met during my first chase of the season.

CHASERCODE

SKYWARN®

A network of volunteers who agree to become the "eyes and ears" of the National Weather Service. Weather spotters provide real-time observations of severe weather events. The Canadian equivalent of SKYWARN® is CANWARN. Most chasers are trained weather spotters and display the SKYWARN® logo on their vehicles.

CHASERCODE

Wall cloud

A large lowering and rotating base of a cumulonimbus cloud that indicates rotation and updraft in a supercell thunderstorm. This part of the storm potentially forms tornadoes. It is typically beneath the rain-free base (RFB) portion of a large thunderstorm at altitudes lower than that of the cloud base. Generally tornadoes will form out of the wall cloud and therefore this becomes the visible target for storm chasers.

CHASERCODE

Mesocyclone

A vortex of air, approximately two to 10 miles in diameter within a large thunderstorm. The mesocyclone features strong surface winds and severe hail. Mesocyclones often occur together with updrafts in supercells, where tornadoes may form.

Funnel cloud developing during the first chase of the season. This was the same storm that produced the Litchfield, IL tornado pictured on the next page.

Photo taken by Chris Thompson

I indicated to Ian and Cody that I wanted to find a place to pull over and get some photos, but Ian noticed that to our right the storm had redeveloped and was again threatening to drop a twister–a distinct lowering was developing–another funnel had begun to form. My truck was about a half mile away–I needed to get closer, but the roads wouldn't allow it. The funnel was roaring across the landscape at about 50 mph, so it was all we could do to keep up with it.

Then it happened: earthly debris arose at the base of the funnel– a tell-tale sign that the tornado was officially on the ground.

We had our first tornado of the year.

Images of the Litchfield, IL tornado (my first intercept of the season) as it crosses Interstate 55.

f2.8
1/320
ISO 1250

CHAPTER 1
INITIATION

ILLINOIS
MISSOURI
TEXAS
ARKANSAS

◉ **REGINA** SK

◉ **BISMARK** ND

◉ **ST. LOUIS** MO
○ **LITCHFIELD** IL

◉ **COLUMBIA** MO

● **SPRINGFIELD** MO

○ **MCALESTER** OK

○ SHERMAN TX

○ BAIRD TX

○ TEXARKANA TX

○ ROLLA MO

◎ LITTLE ROCK AR

○ COAHOMA MI

○ HELENA AR

○ BEEBE AR

○ VELONIA AR

◎ REGINA SK

People ask why I do it. It's a hard question to answer, but you would know it when you experience it. Anyone who has driven a fast car, jumped out of a plane, or free fallen on a carnival ride might understand. Weather is a natural phenomenon that holds a special place for all of us. It's a connection to our physical surroundings that exploits and tantalizes our desire to be a part of the wonder that exists on our planet.

Very little in the natural world produces such violent, yet mysterious, destruction as a tornado. Despite all the warnings in the world, its eventual arrival feels unannounced. As a subject, nothing is as satisfying and as elusive as photographing a good storm.

Developing wall cloud south of Springfield, MO on Day 6 of chasing. It was an uneventful day. This was as close as we came to intercepting a tornado.

f2.8
1/160
ISO 250

APRIL 23, 2011
DAY 7:

We pulled an all-nighter driving back to Columbia. The first tornado intercept of the year—we couldn't have slept if we wanted to. We replayed the storm's story over and over as we congratulated ourselves, proud of our accomplishment.

Forecasts indicated it would be a day or two before the next round of severe weather, so I convinced Ian and Cody to join me for a quick trip to Texas, which looked like it would be busy with storms in the northcentral area. Stopping for fuel in Muskogee, Oklahoma, a convoy pulled into the pumps alongside us—*The Discovery Channel* 'Storm Chasers' crew were taking a pit stop.

Headed in the same direction as we were, radar indicated a line of severe storms had developed along the Red River and were within striking distance. After a quick meet and greet with Reed Timmer, the road trip continued. Now we were part of an even larger convoy of vehicles.

Wall cloud moments before spawning a tornado outside Sherman, TX.

f2.8
1/100
ISO 1600

f2.8
1/200
ISO 2000

With Oklahoma in our rear view mirror, a dramatic green sky loomed overhead, highlighted by a visibly rotating wall cloud. This beautiful Texan storm seemed poised to drop a rope from its jagged base, while at least 40 vehicles positioned themselves under the mesocyclone of this enormous storm.

The Discovery Channel was filming to our right and a deadly, tornado-warned storm was bearing down on us from the left. There was barely enough time to snap a few photos before we had to bolt back to the truck to try and stay in front of the storm. Too late. We were caught in the **bear cage**.

The funnel dropped in front of us with a debris field clearly visible at the ground. Behind us a nasty core of heavy rain and hail was bearing down. Fortunately, the funnel lifted as quickly as it had appeared, providing us with a path to relative safety. Unfortunately, it all happened too quickly and it was too dark to get a decent photo.

CHASERCODE

Bear Cage

A bad spot to be chasing! The bear cage is any area that provides you no route to safety. Generally speaking, when you are caught between two tornadoes, or in our case, between the tornado and a nasty core of rain and hail.

Sherman, TX storm as wall cloud is developing. (above)

Wide view of Sherman, TX storm, shot through the hail-damaged windshield of my truck. (right)

f2.8
1/200
ISO 2000

CHAPTER 1
INITIATION

Large supercell thunderstorm producing a tornado south of Baird, TX. I am positioned approximately three miles east of the storm. (right)

t4
1/400
ISO 200

Fellow chasers analyzing radar data on Day 8 of chasing in northcentral Texas. (left)

DAY 8:
APRIL 24, 2011

The next day we passed through metro Dallas and headed west towards Abilene giving us a great look at the first storm of the day.

Our pursuit took us through back country terrain in the Baird area, and on three separate occasions we stopped to photograph funnels as they developed adjacent to the truck. A dramatic lowering out of the base of the storm made it clear that a tornado was imminent, but as we photographed the scene, the most intense lightning strike imaginable forced us back into the truck. It was so close and so loud that my hair stood up.

This storm produced two tornadoes before dissipating, and provided the backdrop for 'Green Sky Supercell'—one of my favorite images of 2011.

CHASERCODE

Supercell

A thunderstorm that is characterized by the presence of a mesocyclone: a deep, continuously-rotating updraft. Supercells are the least common type of thunderstorm and have the potential to be the most severe. Supercells are often isolated from other thunderstorms, but have dominate the local climate up to 20 miles away.

i3.5
1/80
i90 500

14.5
1/80
ISO 200

Only moments after the top image was taken, a massive lightning strike forced us back into the truck.

This storm produced several tornadoes. Because of darkness, I was forced to shoot at high ISO and wide open at 2.8f. (right)

f2.8
1/160
ISO 1000

*I used a slow shutter to capture the movement of the highway traffic as the storm approached from the west.
(top)*

*The "Green-Sky-Supercell" spawned several funnels and at least two tornadoes. The four images to the right show the development of this beast.
(right)*

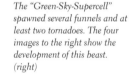

*A funnel cloud developing right over top of our position. This is one of a series of funnels produced by this storm.
(above)*

CHASERCODE

Jungle
There are some parts of the southern United States that see lots of tornadoes but are terrible for chasing. We call these jungles–they feature large hills, giant trees, poor visibility and a road network that is unpredictable. Most common "jungles" are large parts of Arkansas, Louisiana, Missouri, Mississippi and points east.

That evening we met up with a large group of chasers and told stories over burgers and fries (the official meal of storm chasing). Studying numerical models and using various forecasting tools, we agreed that the following few days were going to be huge–but we were also a little worried about terrain. The storms were headed east and that meant hills, trees, wild roads and southern jungle –making chasing almost impossible. We were also concerned with the speed that the storms were expected to travel: fifty to 70 mph ground speed, making chasing virtually inconceivable.

f2.8
1/80
ISO 1600

CHAPTER 1
INITIATION

ILLINOIS
MISSOURI
TEXAS
ARKANSAS

● REGINA SK

● BISMARK ND

● ST. LOUIS MO
○ LITCHFIELD IL

● COLUMBIA MO

● SPRINGFIELD MO

○ MCALESTER OK

● SHERMAN TX

○ BAIRD TX

● TEXARKANA TX

● ROLLA MO

● LITTLE ROCK AR

○ COAHOMA MI

○ HELENA AR

BEEBE AR

VELONIA AR

◉ REGINA SK

APRIL 25 - 27, 2011
DAY 9 - 11:

After a night in Texarkana, there was a day of busted chasing on Arkansas territory that was so brutal I swore I'd never go back. I was tired—really, really tired.

I said goodbye to Ian and Cody and would continue the rest of the way on my own, waking up the next morning in Rolla, Missouri. While loading the last of the camera gear I noticed the truck was leaning to one side. Flat tire. The hotel's complimentary free breakfast had ended at 9:00; it was now 9:15. Please, somebody, give me some good news. Firing up the laptop to find a place to get the tire fixed, I took a peek at the **convective outlook** for the day.

CHASERCODE

Convective Outlook

The Storm Prediction Center issues one to eight-day categorical and probability forecasts for severe weather in the United States. They can be updated up to five times a day.

This was the last of several hundred lightning shots. Five minutes after this shot was taken, I was hiding in a bathtub. It was the morning of April 27. (right)

This photo was taken west of Helena, AR as a tornado-warned storm approached in the dark. (below)

CHASERCODE

Tornado Outbreak

Chasers generally look at any large scale (synoptic) storm system that spawns multiple tornadoes over a one, two or three day period as an outbreak. If a system was to produce a dozen tornadoes or more I would consider it an outbreak. A 'Super Outbreak' (of which there have only been a couple) is when an abnormally large number of tornadoes hits a wide swath of states over a short period of time such as the April 26-28, 2011 Super Outbreak.

Good news at last. Today appeared to have 'historic **tornado outbreak**' written all over it in Arkansas and Mississippi. Didn't I just swear that I would never again chase in Arkansas? The flat fixed, and with a full belly and a travel mug of coffee, I was off again into the jungles of Arkansas. In Little Rock, a quick check of the radar revealed a large number of developing supercells with tornado warnings were headed up Interstate 44.

But, once again Arkansas and its tangled network of roads kicked my ass–I drove and drove and was not able to get into position on any of these very fast-moving storms.

A report began to circulate that one of the storms had just produced a tornado which had directly hit a small town on the Mississippi side of the river. Arriving in Coahoma, Mississippi, 20 minutes after the tornado struck, it was dark, with electricity down and debris scattered everywhere–a very uneasy situation. Emergency vehicles were on scene and groups of people were gathering in the streets. Another huge storm was on its way and I needed to get out of there.

Helena, Arkansas. After a Sonic® burger and checking into a motel, I realized that for all the gas, time driving and mileage I had not taken a single photo all day. Two busted days in a row were not an option, so I decided to head back out on a salvage mission and snap lightning shots while storms were still in the area. I left the radar in the hotel and took my truck for a cruise west of town.

f/7.1
10 sec
ISO 250

Through the darkness it was obvious that a huge storm was developing, with an intense structure visible in the clouds to the south. It looked like a tornado, but was difficult to tell.

Returning to the motel parking lot, tornado sirens began to blare. I rushed back to my room, scanning the radar as the storm sirens continued to howl. A small red box on the screen indicated a tornado warning and I was sitting in the middle of it. I spent the next 20 minutes in the bathroom curled up on the floor of the bathtub. When the storm had passed, I showered and went to bed, only to be jolted awake again by the roar of tornado sirens.

2:15 a.m. The power was out, and I climbed back in the tub, which is where I began the most historic tornado day ever. *CNN* and *The Weather Channel* were warning people throughout the American Southeast that the day was going to be a dangerous one. Analyzing potential targets while continually broadcasting safety guidelines and procedures, the major networks provided wall-to-wall live storm coverage. All indicators pointed to the fact that on that day, a series of storms would produce an abnormally large number of potentially deadly tornadoes.

CHAPTER 1
INITIATION

ILLINOIS
MISSOURI
TEXAS
ARKANSAS

*Storm damage at Beebe, AR
from the same storm that
destroyed Vilonia, AR.
(top left)*

*Tornado damage at Vilonia, AR.
The tornado destroyed 200 homes
and killed four people. I visited
Vilonia on April 27, 2011, the most
prolific tornado day in US history.*

By the end of April 27, 2011, 16 US states felt the impact of 292 tornadoes, resulting in over 300 deaths.

I was still in Arkansas; the chase terrain was poor, the conditions extremely dangerous. It was time to go home—a decision that was difficult but necessary. En route, I stopped to photograph the destruction at Vilonia, Arkansas, at the same time as the Tuscaloosa tornado was wreaking havoc in Alabama. In 1,500 miles I would be back in Saskatchewan.

"We took pictures….so many pictures.
It was a night none of us will ever forget.
Rural Kansas, May, gorgeous storm, epic
lightning and a group of strangers who had
quickly become really close friends…

f2.8
1/320
1250

CHAPTER 2
ENGAGEMENT

NORTH DAKOTA
SOUTH DAKOTA
NEBRASKA
KANSAS
OKLAHOMA

*An early season corn field is
backlit by the passing storm
in central Kansas.*

CHAPTER 2
ENGAGEMENT

MAY 16-18, 2011
DAY 1-3:

Jaclyn on the phone while Martin downloads footage in the back seat. (below)

I spent the first two weeks of May at home in Regina instead of chasing storms. It was a risky decision at the peak of storm season, and if I am being totally honest, it wasn't mine.

f4.5
1/250
ISO 500

My wife was travelling in Europe and I needed to be home with my children. My worst nightmare would have been that those two weeks were extremely busy tornado-wise and I would miss significant photo opportunities.

Luck was on my side. After April 27, 2011 until the middle of May, the jet stream co-operated with my schedule and created conditions that shut down any severe storm potential. I wouldn't have been chasing anyway.

Brent Williamson of *Global Television*, one of the big three networks in Canada, had approached me early in the season about the possibility of having a crew join me for a US storm chase. Jaclyn Whittal was *Global* Regina's broadcast meteorologist and a self-professed weather nerd.

On May 16, 2011, Jaclyn, cameraman Martin Weaver, photographer Vanessa Neufeld and my good friend, storm chaser and flight service specialist (code for 'I know everything about reading weather models') Dallas Hicks piled into my truck and set off on what would become a life-changing experience.

A day and a half of driving and bonding later we found ourselves in Bowdle, South Dakota, thanks to a road detour. Almost exactly one year prior, a monster mile-wide twister had churned past the small village, images from which were broadcast to television sets around the world. We spent several hours in Bowdle, meeting with survivors and listening to their stories of the spiralling terror they had endured.

f4.5
1/2000
ISO 200

Jaclyn in Bowdle, SD, telling the story of the massive twister that just missed the town.

Photo by Vanessa Neufeld

14.5
1/200
ISO 500

Martin preps the camera gear from the back seat while stopped for fuel.

After a gas stop inside Oklahoma we were stopped by State Police for failing to pay for gas.

Photo by Vanessa Neufeld

f3.5
1/30
ISO 640

First order of the day is to check the forecast models. Dallas Hicks works on determining a target for the day's chasing.

CHASERCODE

Enhanced Fujita (EF) Scale

Came into effect in 2007 and replaced the Fujita scale as a means of classification for tornadoes in the US. The scale has six levels from EF0-EF5. It is a damage scale and provides an approximation of wind speeds. Canada still uses the original Fujita Scale.

We continued south toward a developing pattern of severe weather that would produce several EF5 tornadoes with even more destructive power than the one at Bowdle. After a night in North Platte, Nebraska, we headed deeper south through Kansas and into Oklahoma, where a tornado watch in the northcentral part of the state caused chasers to converge as we awaited the development of a storm.

We stopped to fill up at a station in Buffalo, Oklahoma. To keep the pit stops as brief and efficient as possible we each had a role: fuelling the truck, getting drinks, cleaning the windshield or paying for gas. Soon we were on our way, continuing east.

Suddenly, a state police cruiser was roaring up behind us, with the lights on and siren blaring.

Rolling down the window, I asked, "Was I speeding, officer?"

His tone was serious as he peered over my shoulder inside the vehicle. "No," he said, training his gaze back at me over his aviator sunglasses. "However, a vee-hickle matching your description filled up with gas back in Buffalo, and left without paying."

It was Jaclyn's job to pay for the fuel, and in the frantic commotion of the pit stop, she forgot.

I had visions of our chase ending right then and there, but the officer could not have been more understanding. Or talkative. After listening to his very detailed account of the famous Greensburg, Kansas tornado, we paid him for the gas and were on our way.

Pulling up alongside a large group of chasers, we positioned ourselves for the onset of storms. There were several tour groups, including one from the United Kingdom, parked on the side of the road. We gathered more stories and met some great people, but the day was a bust. We were now three days into the chase, and yet to see a storm cloud.

14
1/1250
ISO 640

MAY 19, 2011
DAY 4:

After spending the night in Oklahoma, we began by heading north back to Kansas. The day had potential written all over it—we felt we were perfectly positioned.

We stopped in Pratt, Kansas where we found a motel that would become the base of our operation. Setting up our computers in the lobby, we began to watch and wait. Another group of chasers had the same idea. We struck up an instant friendship and decided to chase as a convoy for the rest of the day.

Brandon, the meteorologist for the other group, along with Dallas and Jaclyn, formulated a plan based on the early radar information and we hit the road.

The developing storms were traveling extremely fast and we had to move as quickly as possible. On two occasions we found ourselves in perfect position, under beautiful supercells at the moment that they showed signs of rotation, but both times the rotation collapsed and the storms fell apart.

From left to right

Large hail is associated with tornado producing storms. The hail in Jaclyn's hand was from Oklahoma.

Dallas and I are checking out the radar and planning a route to our target.

*Photo by
Vanessa Neufeld*

While chasing a storm near Salina, KS, we are passed by another chase vechicle that is fully armor plated...the TIV II, or Tornado Intercept Vehicle Version 2.

CHASERCODE

Rotation
The updraft portion of the storm requires rotation if there is any chance for a tornado. The rotation is visible and is the target area for storm chasers.

f2.8
1/320
ISO 800

f8
1.3s
ISO 800

Allyce kisses her man! After the touchdown of the Manhattan, KS tornado, Ryan got down on a knee and popped the question. (left)

Tornado intercept near Manhattan, KS. (above)

f2.8
1/50
ISO 2500

Dusk, with waning light: parking on the side of a busy highway, unable to go any further east, it was our last hope for the day as we scanned the rapidly moving cloud base for signs of rotation. Screaming and pointing broke out when just over a half mile east a funnel had formed and quickly dropped out of the clouds, appearing to make contact with the ground.

As Martin and I focused our cameras on the tornado, another set of screams erupted, this time for a completely different reason. As the tornado touched down, a member of the other team asked one of his fellow chasers to be his wife. Here we were in Kansas, witnessing a wedding proposal with a tornado on the ground a half mile away.

Couldn't have written a better storm-chasing script.

CHAPTER 2
ENGAGEMENT

NORTH DAKOTA
SOUTH DAKOTA
NEBRASKA
KANSAS
OKLAHOMA

 REGINA SK

 BOWDLE SD

NORTH PLATTE NE

BUFFALO OK

 PRATT KS

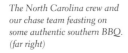 **MANHATTAN** KS

 SALINA KS

WICHITA KS

TULSA OK

ADA OK

ARDMORE OK

JOPLIN MO

Central Kansas provides an excellent mix of storms and chase terrain which makes it perfect for intercepting storms. (above)

Chaser mornings generally consist of checking out of your room, and then gathering to look at weather models and picking a daily target. (right)

The North Carolina crew and our chase team feasting on some authentic southern BBQ. (far right)

Vanessa Neufeld getting the camera ready just prior to our first tornado intercept of this trip. (right)

Martin films Jaclyn as she reports on the story of our first tornado of the trip. (far right)

MAY 20, 2011
DAY 5:

The morning was relaxed; we were already where we needed to be, so there was no need to move until we saw storms developing.

Early that afternoon, the satellite showed a thickening line of cloud cover and a sprinkling of small green orbs popped up on the radar. Vehicles packed, we hit the road, heading south, stopping along the way to photograph a handful of low risk, pretty storms.

The art of storm chasing involves being able to read the weather charts and the radar, blending knowledge and instinct to determine which storms are going to develop into tornado-producing monsters, and which ones are going to die quickly.

East of Pratt, KS we intercepted a storm that we hoped would produce a tornado. It didn't.

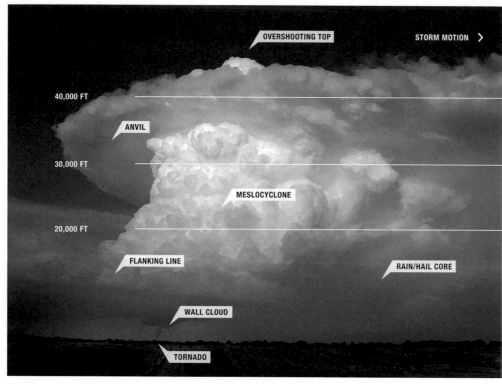

This illustration shows the key features of an **ideal supercell**. These storms generally move from the west to east. Note that the **rain and hail zone** is on the leading edge of the storm. This area is considered the downdraft region or **forward flank downdraft** and is generally positioned toward the northeast portion of the storm. There is a secondary downdraft region called the **rear flank downdraft**. The area where the **wall cloud and tornado** develop is toward the southwest portion of the storm. This area is referred to as the updraft region and is characterized by its **rain-free base** that makes it easy to identify and the rotating **mesocyclone**. Supercells take on an **anvil** shape and they often reach above 50,000 ft in height. There can also be a **flanking line** of smaller cumulus clouds that feed off the updraft of the main storm. When the updraft in a supercell is strong enough, the anvil displays an **overshooting top**…another great indicator for chasers that the storm has potential to produce a tornado.

Using the laptop in one hand, and phone in the other, chasing can be a lot of work. Some days last up to 20 hours when we're on the road. (above)

*Photo by
Vanessa Neufeld*

For this shot I used a small aperture to gain quality and a tripod to prevent camera shake. Despite the look, there was not a breath of wind.

CHAPTER 2
ENGAGEMENT

After a short stop for Jaclyn to broadcast back to the studio in Regina, a supercell storm developed east of our position at Pratt, KS.

Vanessa Neufeld captures lightning strikes in central Kansas.

f10
1/5
ISO 500

The tornado truck with a spider web of intra-cloud lightning providing the backdrop.

Dallas and Jaclyn did a great job of navigating us toward magnificent storms; we eventually ended up in Pratt, Kansas, where we stopped to upload footage and file a report. We were only in the hotel for about 30 minutes before the hail started. A discrete storm had developed unexpectedly behind the primary line of storms. Back on the road, the chase was on. We were loving the fact that we were the only chasers for 50 miles.

We took pictures…so many pictures. It was a night none of us will ever forget. Rural Kansas, May, gorgeous storm, epic lightning and a group of strangers who had quickly become really close friends.

That night we ended up in Wichita, sitting up until 3 a.m. writing, editing, blogging, downloading footage, watching the models and planning for the next day.

MAY 21, 2011
DAY 6:

Jaclyn and I discuss position-ing strategy for the coming chase in Oklahoma.

*Photo by
Vanessa Neufeld*

After a night in Wichita, KS, the day started with blue skies and puffy white clouds (LPF's) but would end with a tornado intercept. (opposite page)

We were up and out of Wichita early. Blasting east, and then south toward Tulsa, Oklahoma, we came across a truck stop with a good road network in all directions, where we decided to wait for the storms to fire up.

It was the day that was supposed to produce our golden nugget. Our spirits had started high, we were well positioned and the Storm Prediction Center was warning of extreme danger. We waited...and waited. Lunch arrived, and then the ice cream. A few puffy clouds floated across the sky. We waited some more.

Dallas and meteorologist Brandon were under fire to provide more information. Is there a better place for us to be? Should we be moving? It was frustrating. The conditions could not have been better for the development of severe weather and tornadoes, but it was getting late and there were no storms to be found.

I was sitting on the grass with my camera when a commotion broke out from the truck, where Dallas, Jaclyn, Brandon and Ryan were huddled over a laptop in heated discussion. A line of storms had popped up on the radar and were heading our direction. But, they were almost 150 miles away and it was already late afternoon. In minutes we were on the road again, with no time to stop–for anything. Watching Martin squirm in the back seat was both funny and painful…he was sweating he had to go so badly.

With every new radar picture, however, it was obvious the storms were developing rapidly and appeared to be producing tornados. Almost immediately after the warnings went up we started getting reports of tornadoes touching down. We couldn't stop, we would miss the show. Poor Martin, he even debated the merits of peeing his pants.

We hadn't had a new radar picture in 20 minutes and the massive, tornado-producing storm seemed to be out of reach for us. Then at the very last possible moment, our radar returned and what we saw was amazing. A new storm had developed–a tornado producer for sure. And, we were only 20 minutes away. We bore down on the storm as it headed directly for us–it was about to drop a tornado. The mesocyclone was rotating rapidly and a beautiful beaver-tail fed the updraft–both hallmarks of a supercell.

The adrenaline was pumping. For Vanessa, Dallas, Jaclyn and Martin this tornado (later dubbed the Ada, Oklahoma tornado) was a first: a textbook storm, from the radar image it was producing to the structure of the clouds. You can read about them all you want, but actually being underneath that kind of rotation is an incredible experience.

CHASERCODE

Storm Prediction Center

Located in Norman, Oklahoma, is tasked with forecasting the risk of severe thunderstorms and tornadoes in the contiguous United States.

Dallas and Martin capture the lowering from the base of rotating wall cloud at Ada, OK. (far left)

Brandon Vincent from Team Red films the touchdown of the first of two tornadoes at Ada, OK. (left)

A wide shot of the Ada tornado as it touches down. There is a large rotating wall cloud visible above the funnel and Vanessa Neufeld is visible in the bottom left corner. (far left)

Jaclyn spots an area of intense rotation associated with this wall cloud. We were at close range and the adrenaline was pumping. (left)

We repositioned several times, and then it happened. The rotating clouds dropped a funnel from the base with a clearly visible debris cloud on the ground. The tornado was backlit by the setting sun. It was beautiful, but it didn't last long. We piled back into the vehicles. Repositioning further east, I could see another funnel descending behind us in the rear view mirror. This tornado lasted longer–it was on the ground for several minutes and seemed to pose for us as it hovered above the road.

As the sun set on Day 6 of the chase, we were on top of the world. Staying up late, we processed images while telling and retelling stories. We had our steak supper that evening, the official meal for tornado hunters after they get their prey.

CHASERCODE

Debris Cloud

Appears beneath a funnel and also circulates around the base of a tornado. The "cloud" of dust or debris is an indicator that the funnel has made contact with the ground.

Following the first tornado we repositioned several times watching the funnel redevelop and dissipate over and over. (right)

f4
1/60
ISO 640

CHAPTER 2
ENGAGEMENT

f2.8
1/15
ISO 1000

f2.8
1/100
ISO1000

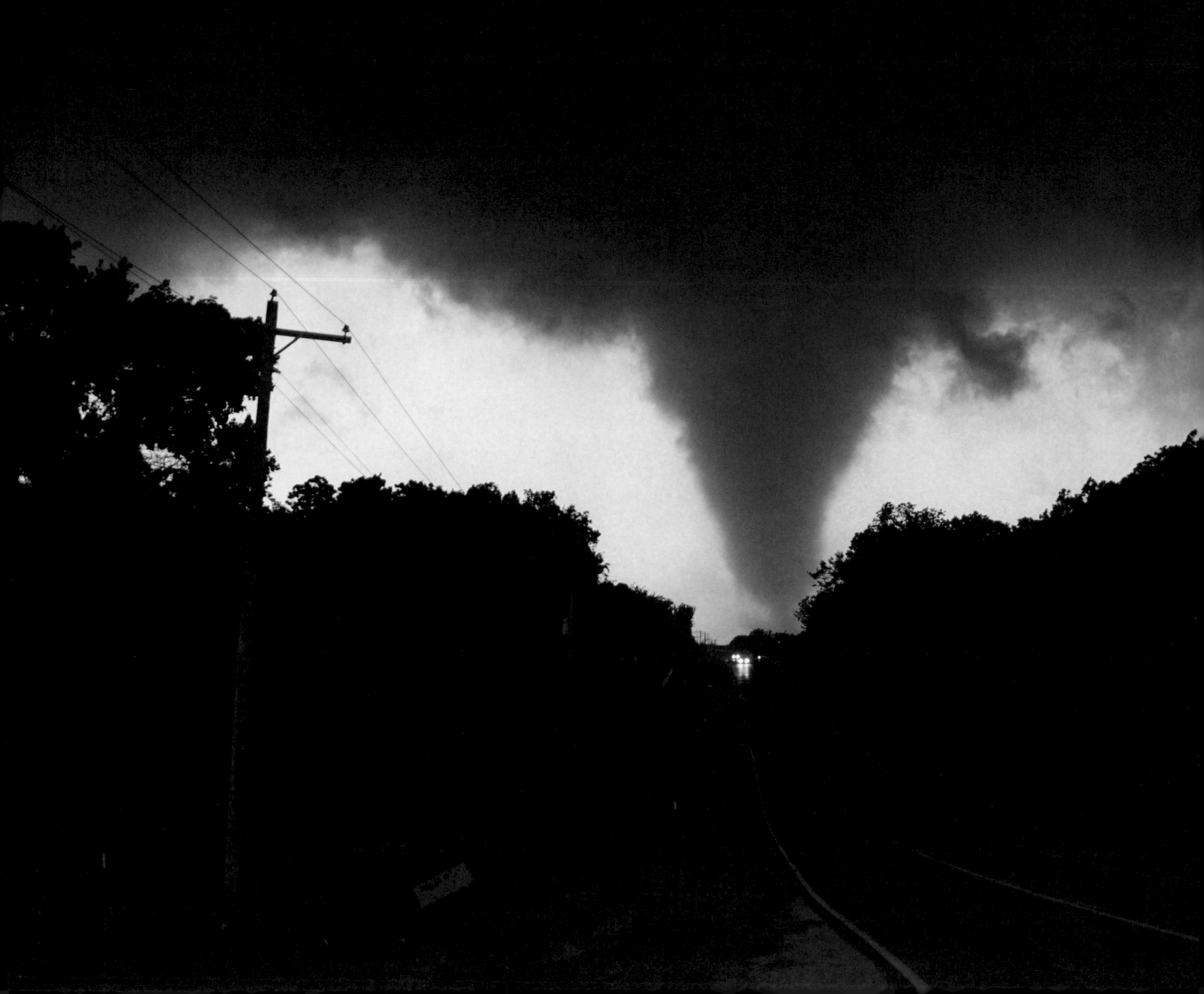

MAY 22, 2011
DAY 7:

The next day was a bust and another great lesson in storm chasing. On this day the atmosphere was ripe. Yesterday was just an appetizer. All of the models pointed to an historic day for tornado development.

Every day there are tough decisions to be made. As the models refined throughout the morning, it became clear that we had a huge one to make. Two areas of interest had developed in Oklahoma, the north play and the south play. The north play—Tulsa, Oklahoma, up to Springfield, Missouri—showed lots of energy, but we weren't certain about a source of lift to get storms started, or the terrain.

Chasing in southern Oklahoma and northern Texas is much better than chasing in the Ozarks east of Tulsa. There was plenty of opportunity for storm development and lots of lift, but the shear (the winds necessary to get a storm rotating) was less than in the north. The terrain was better, however. We headed south, chasing a few weak storms into Texas. As it began to get dark, we headed back into Oklahoma.

On radar we could see that we had made the wrong choice.

Storms were developing on the north play, the Oklahoma-Kansas border. As we watched the radar, the storm continued to grow and a tornado warning was issued. The storm was just out of our daylight range, and we were all very frustrated. The tornado warning box on the radar included the city of Joplin, Missouri—one of my favorite small cities in the United States, and one where I spent time on my very first American storm chase.

Within one hour rumors started circulating about Joplin taking a direct hit. At first we were just annoyed that we had made a bad decision about where to chase, but as the rumors evolved into national news coverage of the complete devastation Joplin had suffered, reality sunk in.

May 22, 2011 was a bust for us, but will go down in history as the day the deadliest tornado in the U.S. in 60 years ravaged Joplin, Missouri.

Previous page

As we repositioned a tornado formed directly behind us, I held the camera over my opposite shoulder and took this shot of it through the door mirror. (left)

We were extremely close to this tornado as it touched down about a third of a mile away. It was heading toward us and we needed to reposition. (right)

CHASERCODE

Tornado Warning

When a tornado is imminent, the National Weather Service in the United States and Environment Canada will issue a warning. The indicators that a tornado is imminent can come from radar information, trained spotters (SKYWARN®) or actual tornado sightings.

CHASERCODE

Bust Day

Chasers refer to a bust when they chase a moderate or high risk day and end up with nothing. The big brother of the Bust day is the 'Blue Sky bust' meaning that not only did you not intercept a tornado but you didn't even get a storm to look at. If the chase day is a low risk day or marginal opportunity that doesn't produce results, it's hard to call it a bust.

12.8
1/80
ISO 1600

The Ada tornado posed over the highway in a gap between trees for several minutes.

"Leaving Canada eight days earlier we had hoped for a tornado intercept or two. What we got was thrust into the middle of the biggest weather story of the year and the deadliest tornado to hit the US in 60 years."

f2.8
1/400
ISO 640

*An iconic image left behind
stands as a symbol of hope and
survival for the people of Joplin.*

CHAPTER 3
JOPLIN

MISSOURI

JOPLIN MO

MAY 22, 2011
DAY 7:

Darkness was falling rapidly, and arriving at the outskirts of Joplin (hours after the tornado ripped through the city) it was clear we were not going to get much further.

The highways were blocked by emergency personnel, debris and overturned vehicles. Attempting to navigate our way in after dark was going to be impossible, so we decided to find hotel rooms nearby and organize our equipment and plan for the morning.

Jaclyn and I had a rough night. We hadn't slept; emotionally and physically we were exhausted. *Global National News* had yanked Jaclyn and Martin off our crew entirely to report solely on the Joplin disaster for the next few days. Jaclyn was stressed, a rookie television weather specialist, she was trained to forecast weather in Canada. Now she was about to cover the lead story on a national broadcast from a disaster zone.

Furious that our team was being split up, I didn't help matters much. Things boiled over and we had a heated exchange before parting ways.

It was the last we spoke for days. Dallas, Vanessa and I were on our own.

Arriving back at Joplin's city limits in the early morning hours, we saw right away that the problem was finding a way in. Relying on landmarks wasn't possible as roads were blocked and street signs had vanished, ripped off their posts. We managed to maneuver past a barricaded ramp and pressed deeper into the city. Broken tree limbs and missing shingles soon gave way to homes missing roofs and overturned vehicles. Moving slowly towards the city center, the scene unfolding in front of us was apocalyptic.

Nothing was where it was supposed to be. Cars were on their roofs, buildings and homes lay far from their foundations, or crumpled where they once stood like piles of matchsticks. Moving past a police checkpoint, we found ourselves in the heart of the hardest hit neighborhoods. The Tornado Truck inched slowly through the rubble. Our goal was to make it to the site of the local hospital, which had reportedly been destroyed.

Joplin, Missouri was completely devastated by an EF5 tornado on May 22, 2011. (opposite page)

Wind speeds in excess of 250 mph stripped bark from trees and threw vehicles for hundreds of yards.

CHAPTER 3
JOPLIN

MISSOURI

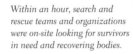

JOPLIN MO

The tornado made a direct hit on the heart of the city of Joplin, leaving behind a damage path almost 12 miles long. (opposite page)

Within an hour, search and rescue teams and organizations were on-site looking for survivors in need and recovering bodies.

Members of search and rescue discover a body in the rubble... one of more than 150 that perished due to this monster storm.

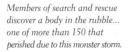

f2.8
1/320
ISO 640

St. John's Regional Medical Center bore a direct hit from the tornado and sustained such damage that it is has since been demolished. (top left)

In the parking lot of St. John's Regional Medical Center cars were piled like toys in a box. (bottom left)

The air ambulance destroyed in the parking lot of the hospital. This image was on the cover of several Canadian newspapers the next morning. (left)

The wreck of St. John's Regional Medical Center in the background and complete destruction in the foreground. Prosthetics litter the road across from the hospital. (top right)

Destruction was everywhere and we had to pass through a couple of police checkpoints before we were able to get into the city. (bottom right)

CHAPTER 3
JOPLIN

MISSOURI

JOPLIN MO

During the early hours after the tornado struck reports circulated of EF4 level damage, this was later upgraded and confirmed as EF5 damage.

The steel skeleton of a gas station canopy, twisted and crushed, displays the raw power of this incredible storm.

Looking east from the hospital parking lot the path of the tornado is painfully obvious. (right)

In every direction the destruction was absolute; the landscape unrecognizable with the exception of the shell of the hospital looming in the distance. The one mile trek from the checkpoint to the hospital felt like a million. Beside us, a team of search and rescue professionals pulled bodies from the wreckage. We were awake in a nightmare. As the media calls started pouring in, I switched my phone off, still trying to process the scene in front of me. Vanessa was in tears. We held onto each other and cried; at that moment it was all we could do.

Two things struck me that morning as we photographed the city: the sound, and the smell. I expected chaos, sirens blaring, frantic search and rescue teams yelling at each other as they tore through rubble looking for survivors. Instead it was quiet, eerily so. Vehicles crept by, a generator purred here and there, people spoke in hushed tones.

Small groups of stunned residents moved furtively through the streets, stopping occasionally to look around them in disbelief. Others just stood in place, holding hands or hugging. Exhausted fire fighters, police and first responders knelt silently, mustering the strength to continue.

And the smell. It was the same odor that fills the air immediately after a torrential downpour, sharpened by the acrid fumes of gasoline. I won't ever forget it.

The next morning, my photo of the helicopter and hospital ran on the front page of Saskatchewan newspapers. Joplin was a disaster zone filling up with emergency personnel. Our intention when we arrived was to do whatever we could to help, but given the magnitude of the destruction, we were just not properly equipped. There was no apparent central command post for volunteers, so despite the fact that every fiber of my being wanted to stay and assist, we all agreed that we should leave Joplin and let the professionals do their work.

The drive west into Oklahoma was subdued. I sat in the front passenger seat reviewing images from Joplin, while Vanessa did the same in the back seat. There was no music playing. Occasionally Vanessa or I would offer up a photo as we discussed what we had just witnessed, over and over. Our roller-coaster of emotions had just hit the very bottom; only 40 hours earlier the five of us had been giddy and celebrating as we intercepted the two tornadoes in Oklahoma.

I have heard reports that it took only 45 seconds for the tornado to pass over any given point on its destructive path. (top left)

Within hours television news mobile units were on scene relaying the images and stories from Joplin. (bottom left)

Any trees that were not completely destroyed had the leaves, branches and bark sandblasted away in a matter of seconds. (right)

It was almost impossible to distinguish where one property or home ended and the next began. (right)

The damage path extended for as far as the eye could see. Cars were thrown like toys and homes were leveled down to their foundations. (right)

An American flag lies in tatters in the rubble of a well-built brick building. (left)

Jaclyn and Martin spent three days in Joplin, broadcasting the tragedy back to Canadians. *Global National News* made the right decision to pull them away from us; we would have been a distraction. Leaving Canada eight days earlier we had hoped for a tornado intercept or two. What we got was thrust into the middle of the biggest weather story of the year and the deadliest tornado to hit the US in 60 years.

"The tornado watch was replaced with a warning and as the storm came into view it appeared obvious that it was a beast capable of spawning a tornado."

CHAPTER 4
CRUSHING DEFEAT

OKLAHOMA

KANSAS

f2.8
1/250
ISO 1250

Oklahoma is the land of plenty when it comes to tornadoes. This amazing storm developed north of Enid, OK.

I usually sit in the passenger seat with camera at the ready. When we stop I pop out and set up quickly. We may only stop for a few seconds or just a few minutes.

*Photo by
Vanessa Neufeld*

MAY 22, 2011
DAY 7:

The mood was different in the truck, but by the time we had made our way out of Joplin, new storms were already gathering. It was clear that we were going to have to move east quickly to get into position for another round of storms.

CHASERCODE

Intercept

Any time that a chaser can get reasonably close to a tornado we call it an intercept. It means something a bit different to every chaser.

Oklahoma is the Promised Land when it comes to tornadoes, with its potent mix of good chase terrain and conditions suitable for producing twisters virtually 12 months of the year. Our target area was west of Interstate 35 where we hoped to intercept a line of storms that had developed near Enid, Oklahoma and were moving along the same general line as storms from the day before.

We were receiving reports of large hail and time was not on our side. The tornado watch was replaced with a warning and as the storm came into view it appeared obvious that it was a beast capable of spawning a tornado. We quickly found a dirt road that would put us in position in front of the rotating mesocyclone. A year earlier

I had intercepted a tornado very close to this same area, which had produced the largest hail I had ever seen. I felt good about our chances for a repeat performance.

We watched and waited, then repositioned. We repositioned again. The storm was about to overtake us so we repositioned one last time. The tornado never did appear. During previous chases it was always disappointing if the storm didn't produce a twister. This time felt a bit different. Joplin was still very fresh in our minds and we were totally drained. It was the earliest night we had during that trip. We found a motel in Ponca City, Oklahoma, opened a bottle and settled in front of the television to watch the ongoing coverage from Joplin.

As we approached the storm, the tornado warning went up on our radar screen. This storm looked very intense.

f2.8
1/400
ISO 400

CHAPTER 4
CRUSHING DEFEAT

The wall cloud of this tornado-warned storm passes over a large group of chasers. (above)

f2.8
1/60
ISO 1250

MAY 23, 2011
DAY 8:

The death toll from Missouri was climbing and during the night at least one serious storm had rumbled through the Joplin area, triggering tornado warning rumors amongst traumatized local residents.

CHASERCODE

Particularly Dangerous Situation (PDS)

The Storm Prediction Center issues a PDS (Particularly Dangerous Situation) on the very rare occasions when probabilities of large destructive tornadoes are extremely high.

Early that morning the threat level for another outbreak of tornadoes was considered high. In fact the Storm Prediction Centre went so far as to declare this threat a Particularly Dangerous Situation (PDS), with explosive supercells anticipated. The Centre warned that tornadoes could be of the destructive variety, generating hail up to three inches in diameter. Central Oklahoma predominated the threat zone, with the metropolitan Oklahoma City area lying smack in the cross-hair.

We were well positioned for these storms. Mid-afternoon we hooked back up with our friends from North Carolina on a rural highway northwest of Oklahoma City. A significant storm had developed and, according to the radar, was getting ready to unleash its deadly fury.

As it sometimes happens, the roads, towns, construction and speed of the storm conspired to drive us out of position. We were propelled in front of the massive core of the cell and could not risk driving blind into its belly. We stayed ahead of it, trying desperately to find an opening that would allow us to get around to the storm's west side. By the time we managed to do so, it was too late.

f2.8
1/160
ISO 2500

We repositioned several times as the storm threatened to drop a tornado in front of us. It became very dark so I moved the ISO up to 2500 to get a decent shutter speed. (above)

This storm had all of the ingredients. It came close, we saw lots of rotation in the wall cloud, but it never did produce. (bottom left)

Vanessa taking photos of this intense storm as it passed to our north. It was great having another photographer on the trip.(bottom right)

f2.8
1/2500
ISO 400

f2.8
1/400
ISO 400

CHAPTER 4
CRUSHING DEFEAT

OKLAHOMA
KANSAS

● **JOPLIN** MO

● **ENID** OK

○ **PONCA CITY** OK

○ **OKLAHOMA CITY** OK

● **SHAWNEE** OK

● **READING** KS

f2.8
1/25
ISO 1250

We were so worried about this town, there was a tornado warning on radar from the SPC and the storm sirens were not going off.

The massive EF5 tornadoes did considerable damage in the Oklahoma City area and as darkness fell, the remnants of the storm were headed again into southwestern Missouri, towards Joplin. On May 24, 2011, 57 tornadoes were reported in six states. We saw none of them.

It was a rather anti-climactic chase to end this tour. We were completely exhausted and ready for rest. After one last night in Oklahoma, Dallas and I said good-bye to the North Carolina team, and to Vanessa, who was headed to Texas for some down time. The next morning Dallas and I began the long drive back to Saskatchewan. On the way we stopped in Reading, Kansas, where just a few days earlier a tornado had ripped through the town while we were filming our tornado in Ada, Oklahoma.

Different town, same result–200 homes damaged or destroyed and lives changed forever. Despite the warnings and the preparedness of the community, one man was killed. One last reminder as we journeyed home of the power of this natural phenomenon.

Reading, Kansas was a disaster zone. Close to 200 structures were damaged or completely destroyed. This was our last stop on this incredible tour through Tornado Alley.

f2.8
1/5000
ISO 400

f5
5sec
ISO 200

St Paul, NE was the last s
of the day. The light show
was intense directly overhe
Here the water tower is
illuminated with multiple
lightning strikes.

CHAPTER 5
**GUSTNADOES
IN NEBRASKA**

SOUTH DAKOTA
NEBRASKA

◉ **REGINA** SK

● **MITCHELL** SD

○ **TAYLOR** NE

○ ST. PAUL NE

MAY 29, 2011

The mesocyclone passed by with a visibly rotating wall cloud that headed northeast over ranch land. A tornado was reported 10 minutes after this photo was taken about 10 miles east. There were no roads so we could not chase. (right)

Even though it was still a few days away, conditions for May 30, 2011 looked great for South Dakota, and I was determined not to miss out.

Accompanied by my good friend and fellow chaser Notanee Bourassa, I left Regina early on the morning of May 29, 2011. Our target was southcentral South Dakota, but as we wound our way in that direction, it shifted to the east. We ended up spending the night in Mitchell South Dakota, where we were hit with a hail storm five minutes after checking into our room.

Waking up bright and early in the middle of our new target zone, we spent the morning prepping camera gear and watching the radar for early signs of initiation. Satellite imagery showed a line of cloud developing in Nebraska, so we opted to continue moving south toward it.

We made the right decision, eventually ending up on the dangerous side of a great storm which was throwing down huge hail. The problem: the road network was not going to allow us to go where we needed to go to follow this storm.

We were at a crossroads: move forward towards the next storm (no guarantees), or drive back through a massive hail-producing monster. We decided to stay south and east of the storm and wait for the next line to develop.

We were not alone–the storm chaser convergence was insane. Ending up in a group of about 20 vehicles, we were passed from the opposite direction by about as many vehicles again. We pulled over and waited it out alongside chasing legends like Mark Robinson and Scott McPartland, but the rotating storm we were looking for was not showing up.

Notanee and I met up with some familiar faces near Taylor, NE. Dayna Vetesse, Mark Robinson, Scott McPartland, Daniel Shaw and Dave Lewison as well as about 20 others that I did not know. (bottom)

CHASERCODE

Initiation

When chasers are watching radar early in a chase day we are looking for any radar indication of a storm developing.

CHASERCODE

Chaser Convergence

Sometimes one storm stands out among the crowd and all the chasers end up in the same area. At times the convergence causes traffic jams and slows down everyone. Convergence is worse on weekends and when the storms are close to the large metropolitan areas such as Dallas, Oklahoma City, Wichita and Kansas City.

f2.8
1/400
ISO 400

We repositioned further south just in time for the next cell that developed. (left)

12.6
1/800
ISO 640

Gas stop at Taylor, NE where we separated. For most of the chaser group the day was done. For Notanee and I this was just the beginning. (right)

f3.5
1/640
ISO 500

Our chase group stopped for about 20 minutes as the storm fell apart. We looked at the radar to determine what our next move would be. (right)

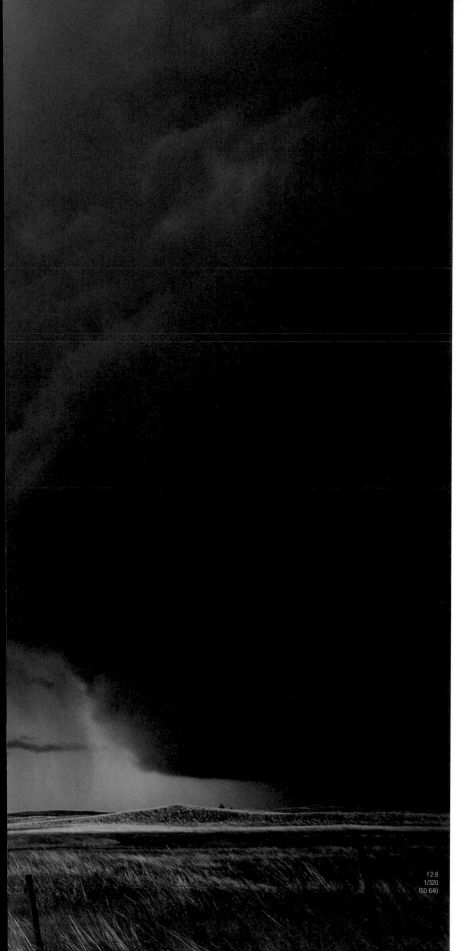

f 2.8
1/320
ISO 640

Ten miles north of Taylor, NE, Notanee Bourassa and I watch a developing wall cloud moving toward our position. This image was shot as part of a time-lapse sequence with a tripod mounted camera.(right)

f4
1/250
ISO 200

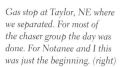

CHAPTER 5
**GUSTNADOES
IN NEBRASKA**

SOUTH DAKOTA
NEBRASKA

◉ **REGINA** SK

● **MITCHELL** SD

○ **TAYLOR** NE

○ ST. PAUL NE

◉ REGINA SK

The gust front with an associated "gustnado" appears ready to engulf a farmyard in rural Nebraska. (right)

f3.2
1/320
ISO 500

We blasted south from Taylor and were stopped in our tracks by what looked like a funnel developing right in front of us. (left)

f2.8
1/320
ISO 2500

On several occasions we got caught in debris fields from strong down-bursts associated with this storm. (left)

f2.8
1/320
ISO 2500

f2.8
1/320
ISO 2500

We witnessed several funnels with associated debris clouds at the ground. This image is facing east, the storm is behind us heading east. We are between the rain core and the gust front. This was an intense drive. (above)

On at least four occasions we were rocked by intense winds in the 80 mph range. (left)

Everyone agreed that the radar picture was not looking great–no longer a line of discrete storms; instead a long mass of rain and hail stretched about 150 miles from its north to south edges. It was headed east and we were out in front of it. Most crews decided to get gas and start heading back. Except us. Notanee and I had come a long way and were not ready to give up. Most of the other chasers had ended their day, so we were now the lone chase vehicle on a very lonely rural Nebraska highway.

With only about an hour of daylight left and the help of the radar and the map, we found what looked to be a promising area that showed some intense rotation. We were off, heading south and then east. Stopping to get some photos of a menacing cloud bank, I noticed what Notanee and I initially agreed looked like smoke rising from the ground, but soon realized was debris.

CHAPTER 5
GUSTNADOES
IN NEBRASKA

SOUTH DAKOTA
NEBRASKA

⊙ **REGINA** SK

● **MITCHELL** SD

○ **TAYLOR** NE

○ **ST. PAUL** NE

⊙ REGINA SK

f2.8
1/320
ISO 2500

The spin-ups seemed to be happening all around us. The storm was traveling incredibly fast so most of these images are shot from the car. (left)

f2.8
1/80
ISO 400

Some of the tell-tale signs of "gustnadoes" are the lack of a visible funnel at the cloud base and the rather loosely organized debris cloud. We saw plenty of them on this day.

f/4.5
1/5
ISO 500

As darkness descended the intensity of the winds increased. This image shows a large area of debris being kicked up directly in front of us. A tornado was reported with associated damage about a mile to the south.

CHASERCODE

Gustnadoes

A short-lived, low-level rotating cloud that can form in a severe thunderstorm. They form in the downdraft from the gust (outflow) front of a strong thunderstorm. Bit of a slang term.

Moving east and over the course of the next half hour, we witnessed no less than 15 gustnadoes, some at very close range. On two occasions we found ourselves trapped in the debris field with winds in excess of 90 mph, shaking our truck off its tires.

Finally, as the last echoes of light drained off the horizon we witnessed what we believe was a tornado (and was later reported as such by trained spotters west of St. Paul, Nebraska). When we finally got to town the sirens were wailing and the area was under a tornado warning.

It was then that I took some of my favorite lightning shots of the year. The town was littered with debris, numerous trees were down and homes were damaged. We received reports of a tornado in the area from a frantic man who stopped us and asked us for help in finding emergency personnel.

At the end of the day, 23 tornadoes had touched down, and we ended up right in the middle of it all.

When the sirens fired up my position could not have been better. There was very little chaser traffic and the atmospheric conditions screamed 'tornado!'"

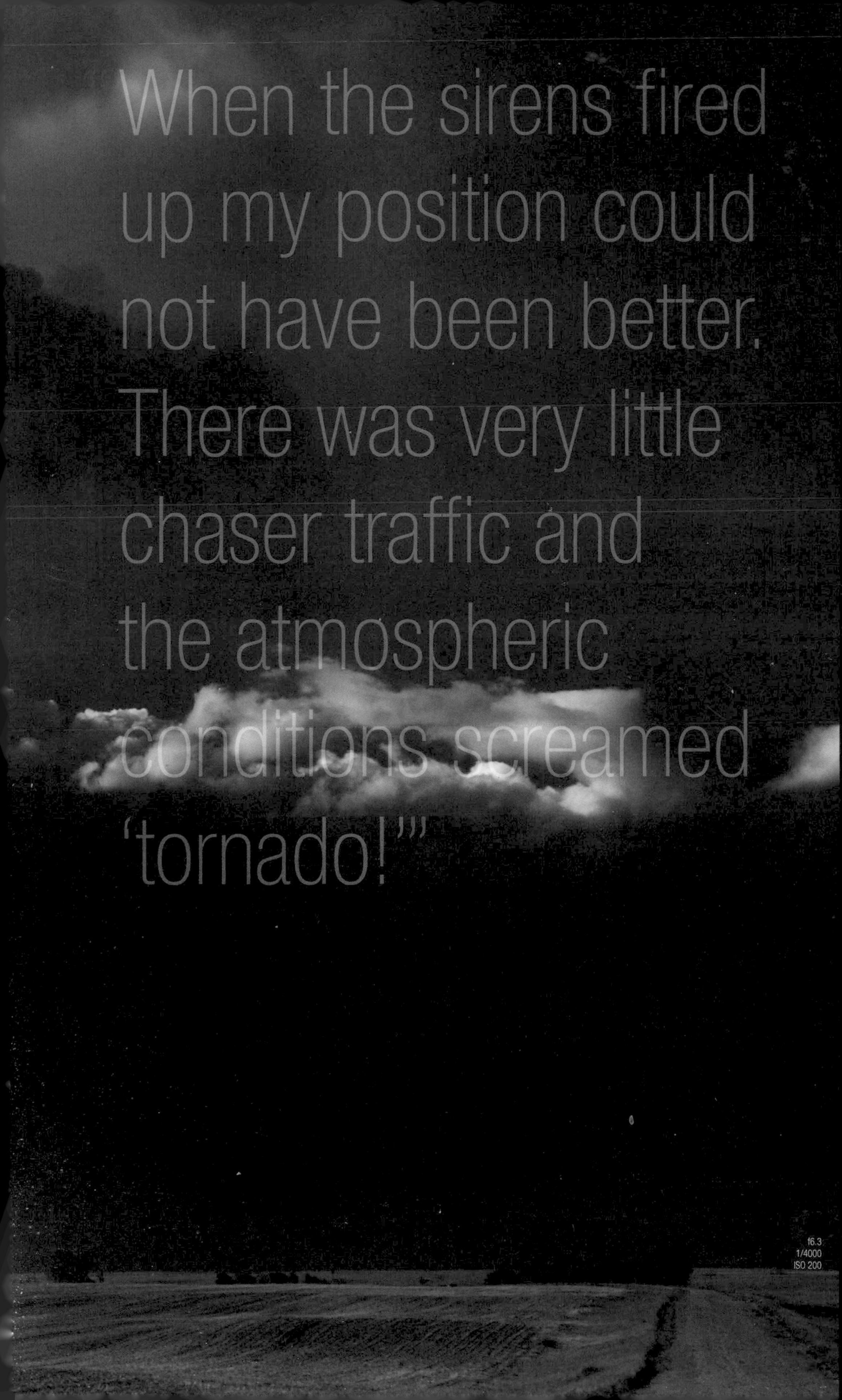
f6.3
1/4000
ISO 200

CHAPTER 6

MONTANA MONSTER

MONTANA
NORTH DAKOTA

East of Bismarck, ND, a storm develops and quickly becomes tornado-warned. I was one of only two chasers in the area.

JUNE 6, 2011

CHASERCODE

Tornado Alley

For chasers, this is a well-defined corridor through the central US that includes the plains states of Texas, Oklahoma, Kansas, Nebraska, South Dakota, North Dakota and into parts of Saskatchewan and Manitoba. There are numerous other states that from year to year produce more numerous and/or deadly tornadoes. However part of the significance of Tornado Alley is the ability to chase in terrain that provides good roads and visibility and a reasonably predictable pattern of timing from year to year.

As the season progresses, the location of serious storms tends to course north and west. The 2011 season was a perfect reflection of this trend. As the storm season began, the April tornado count in the southeast United States was historic. Then, as June approached, warnings and storms began popping up throughout the Dakotas, Colorado, Wyoming and Montana.

As it turned out, North Dakota was indeed a very busy district of 2011's Tornado Alley. Before we get to that, let me tell you about my most dangerous storm chasing experience, which happened May 24, 2010 at Elgin, North Dakota...

Chasing alone, on a day that had outbreak written all over it, was not a great idea. Earlier in the day I was chasing in the Howes/Faith, South Dakota area, and experienced several tornadoes—my photos of that event are some of my favorite. Heading toward home, the storms continued to shows signs of rotation. I found myself alone on Highway 21, west of Elgin, under a rotating mesocyclone which dropped a funnel on the road directly in front of me. Forced to put my truck in reverse and speed backwards away from the approaching funnel, I was alone in the middle of nowhere, and in trouble.

An election sign lifted out of the ditch and flew through the air beside me as the twister lifted and briefly disappeared. Seizing the opportunity, I spun the car around and blasted east as fast as I could. Seconds later it dropped again, this time in the field to my left.

f2.8
1/1600
ISO 800

Early afternoon in northeast Montana. Storms firing up and I am on my way to Billings, MT. (opposite page)

I could see this storm from about 60 miles away. As I came over a hill and Billings came into view this was the scene that greeted me. (above)

I snapped a couple of photos as the tornado continued to grow less than 200 yards away, finally disappearing up over the hills and into the rain. North Dakota would have a hard time living up to that kind of memory in 2011.

I only had one chase opportunity in the Peace Garden State, a quick two-day chase that began near Billings, Montana. It was early June and what might have been the most picturesque, perfectly formed supercell I have ever seen presented itself southwest of the city.

f2.8
1/30
ISO 400

A close call as a funnel touched down in the field beside me. This was near Elgin, North Dakota. (left)

f2.8
1/50
ISO 800

f2.8
1/30
ISO 400

f2.8
1/50
ISO 2000

f2.8
1/50
ISO 800

Just west of Billings, MT, a wall cloud passes overhead. Several small spin-ups were visible near the ground and one passed extremely close to me, evidenced by the broken street sign in the foreground. Note in the photo above (taken minutes prior) that the sign is intact. (left and top)

The wall cloud continues to spin away from my position, eventually producing a tornado after dark. (bottom left)

The Billings storm continued to grow as darkness approached. Note that the ISO here had crept up to 2000. (bottom right)

CHASERCODE

Twister

Twister, tornado...You say potato. These are interchangeable, however twister is definitely considered slang.

When the sirens fired up my position could not have been better. There was very little chaser traffic and the atmospheric conditions screamed "tornado!" The day had started very early in Saskatchewan and ended in Montana, and encompassed almost 500 miles and 3,000 photos. It had been a long day and I was alone in the truck.

When this amazing supercell showed itself on the horizon, the payoff seemed worth all the driving. The movement in the clouds was intense, eventually producing a tornado near a city that still had fresh wounds from a year earlier when a destructive twister took direct aim at the Billings Heights region.

CHAPTER 6
MONTANA MONSTER

MONTANA
NORTH DAKOTA

 REGINA SK

 BILLINGS MT

 MILES CITY MT

 BISMARK ND

 JAMESTOWN ND

 REGINA SK

After dark, the storm moved off to the east producing near constant lightning. I needed to get to North Dakota by morning but stopped several times to photograph the light show. (left)

The storm was moving quickly and stayed in front of me, hovering over the interstate. Anvil crawling lightning made its way up and down the rear flank of the cloud. (below)

The system was moving east and the outlook for North Dakota within the next 24 hours was also very potent. I would have to get as far east as I could overnight. I met up with fellow chaser Daniel Shaw from Australia–a guy who puts more miles on while chasing storms than anyone I know. Daniel would be my comic relief and travel companion for the following day.

We traveled behind the storm as it moved toward the border. The light show was simply amazing, with **intra-cloud lightning** repeatedly crawling up the west wall of the supercell. We were confident that the next day would be a good one. The chase ended late and I picked up the last room at the motel.

CHASERCODE

Intra-Cloud Lightning

Occurs between areas of differing electric potential within a single cloud. Intra-cloud lightning is the most frequently occurring type.

f5.6
3sec
ISO 500

f5.6
2sec
ISO 500

CHAPTER 6
MONTANA MONSTER

MONTANA
NORTH DAKOTA

◉ **REGINA** SK

◉ **BILLINGS** MT

● **MILES CITY** MT

◉ **BISMARK** ND

◎ JAMESTOWN ND

◎ REGINA SK

f6.3
1/1600
ISO 500

JUNE 7, 2011

Morning came early. The truck was gassed and I was fed and on the road by 10:00 a.m. After just four hours on the road the radar indicated that storms were beginning to develop southwest of Bismarck. The chase was on.

CHASERCODE

Squall Lines/ Derechos

A line of severe thunderstorms that form along or ahead of a cold front. It contains heavy precipitation, hail, lightning, strong straight-line winds, and possibly tornadoes. A derecho (which is similar in structure) tends to be longer lived and have sustained winds at or above 58 mph as opposed to gusts.

Many of the storms and the systems that produced tornadoes in 2011 were large, fast systems that brought together multiple supercells, eventually blending into large lines of storms called Squall lines or derechos. This day in North Dakota was different–developing storms had two unique and desirable characteristics. First, the storms were very slow moving, in the neighborhood of five to 10 mph. Secondly, each storm was distinct and separate from the next, easily viewable from a distance without any clouds obstructing the view.

Storms began firing up early in the afternoon just south of Bismarck. I was in perfect position. (above)

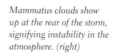

f4.5
1/1600
ISO 320

Mammatus clouds show up at the rear of the storm, signifying instability in the atmosphere. (right)

North Dakota is excellent
chase terrain with a good
gridded road network and
open skies and fields.

f6.3
1/3200
ISO 500

The storm continued
to build throughout the
afternoon until finally a
tornado warning was issued.

f6.3
1/2500
ISO 320

CHAPTER 6
MONTANA MONSTER

MONTANA
NORTH DAKOTA

 REGINA SK

BILLINGS MT

MILES CITY MT

 BISMARK ND

JAMESTOWN ND

REGINA SK

Just before sunset the storm began to fall apart and the warning was dropped without a sighting of a tornado.

The east-west road ended and now I had to make my move north. Time for just a couple more photos before the rain closed in.

f4.5
1/500
ISO 320

The last pic of the day as the sun prepares to set. The storm was falling apart and the chase was done. Next stop, Mexican food in Jamestown.

CHASERCODE

Tornado Potential

Potential comes in the form of Slight, Moderate and High risk. Tornadoes can develop out of any severe thunderstorm but conditions vary. The combination of variables defines the threat level.

The added benefit was that because that day was considered marginal for tornado potential, many chasers saved the gas and stayed home. So, Daniel and I found ourselves under a perfect discrete supercell, all alone. A red warning box flashed on the screen and there we were, sitting underneath that day's only North American storm with a tornado warning.

We watched as the storm rotated and threatened to produce. We repositioned over and over to stay under the danger zone, but the warning finally subsided and the chase was called.

Daniel headed south toward Kansas, and I was on my way home again.

"A 300-yard-wide rain obscured twister churned across the ranch land to our north, however, due to the poor road network in the area we could not continue to chase."

14.5
1/50
ISO 250

CHAPTER 7
LOOKING FOR SOUTH DAKOTA MAGIC

SOUTH DAKOTA
WYOMING
MONTANA
NORTH DAKOTA

*The lowering crosses the road
in front of us. A 300-yard-wide
rain-wrapped tornado developed
about 10 minutes later over
ranch land to our east.*

CHAPTER 7
**LOOKING FOR SOUTH
DAKOTA MAGIC**

f4.5
1/50
ISO 250

JUNE 12, 2011

One of my favorite places to chase storms is South Dakota. The views are spectacular, the towns are friendly and hospitable, motels are inexpensive and the tornadoes are epictacular. The SPC had placed a big 'Moderate Risk' button over the northwest region of the state, and that was good enough to get our juices going.

An elephant trunk tornado between Faith and Howes, SD on May 24, 2010. This was one of a half dozen tornadoes that day and the reason I love South Dakota so much.

I just crossed the border into Montana when the tornado warning was issued on this storm near Alzada.

I spent a night in North Dakota, heading out in the morning toward my initial target of Faith, South Dakota. It seemed like a good location with roads for storm pursuit heading in all directions. I was also a bit nostalgic for the place, considering I had seen six tornadoes there a year ago.

On May 24, 2010, the storm that had produced tornadoes in the Howes and Faith, South Dakota, region was discrete, enormous and terrifying. Fate and the radar had landed me at a gas station in Faith watching a small storm develop very close to town. I was trying to get some shots of the structure of the storm when sirens started blaring. It was a little shocking because only a few minutes before the last radar picture had not indicated any tornado potential. A quick check of the radar revealed that it was not the storm in front of me that was raising the alarms, but rather a new storm that was approaching from south of town.

14.5
1/800
ISO 250

f4.5
1/60
ISO 250

It was very painful watching this storm move off to the east knowing that it was poised to produce a tornado.

CHASERCODE

Tornado Types

Tornadoes come in all sorts of colors, shapes and sizes ranging from near 100 feet wide at the base to as large as over a mile wide. The common chaser descriptions are Wedge, Elephant Trunk, Rope, Cone and Stove Pipe to match the shapes that each exhibits. The color generally depends on the type of terrain and the moisture level present when the tornado develops.

WEDGE

STOVEPIPE

ROPE

ELEPHANTTRUNK

CONE

Back in the Belle Fourche area. This was our last chance at an intercept. Unfortunately we had to go too far south and were now out of position.

Jetting south from Faith toward Howes, the storm came quickly into focus. It was beautiful and perfect. A large wedge-shaped tornado was on the ground and clearly visible even from my distance of about 10 miles away. When I got within a couple of miles of the twister, I pulled over and started shooting. Over the next hour or so, and after several changes in location, that monster storm produced six tornadoes.

What was truly incredible about this event was that all categories of tornado were on display. The first was the massive 500-yard-wide wedge, followed by a classic cone-shaped tornado that morphed into a perfect rope from cloud to ground. Then a perfect elephant trunk played in the open field for several minutes before dissipating. After a brief quiet spell the storm finally produced a perfect stovepipe tornado—a bit more difficult to see due to the hail and rain, but I managed to get a few photos.

CHAPTER 7
**LOOKING FOR SOUTH
DAKOTA MAGIC**

SOUTH DAKOTA
WYOMING
MONTANA
NORTH DAKOTA

 REGINA SK

● **WILLISTON** ND

○ **FAITH** SD

○ **BELLE FOURCHE** SD

○ **ALZADA** MT

○ REGINA SK

f10
1/2
ISO 320

CHAPTER 7
LOOKING FOR SOUTH DAKOTA MAGIC

SOUTH DAKOTA
WYOMING
MONTANA
NORTH DAKOTA

◉ **REGINA** SK

● **WILLISTON** ND

○ **FAITH** SD

○ **BELLE FOURCHE** SD

○ **ALZADA** MT

f3.5
1/30
ISO 500

Sunset on the high plains. Now the hard part, the long drive back to Saskatchewan. Notanee and I stopped in North Dakota and slept in our vehicles for a few hours.

During the overnight drive home though the Dakotas, several thunderstorms crossed our path.

One year later, I was hoping for a repeat of this type of storm again in 2011.

Throughout the day all indications were that the system was going to start firing up further west than was originally anticipated. After repositioning closer to the Wyoming border, I met up with Notanee Bourassa. We shot northwest through Wyoming and into Montana where we met up with a large group of chasers as the primary storm of the day crossed the highway in front of us.

A tornado warning was issued, and a 300-yard-wide rain-obscured twister churned across the ranch land to our north. But, thanks to the poor road network in the area, we could not continue to chase and had to travel almost 50 miles in another direction, ending our day early. All was not lost, however. There were other smaller storms in the area, and I salvaged the opportunity by capturing some beautiful lighting images.

"That night wrapped up in Holdrege, Nebraska, with a lightning display the likes of which none of us had ever seen."

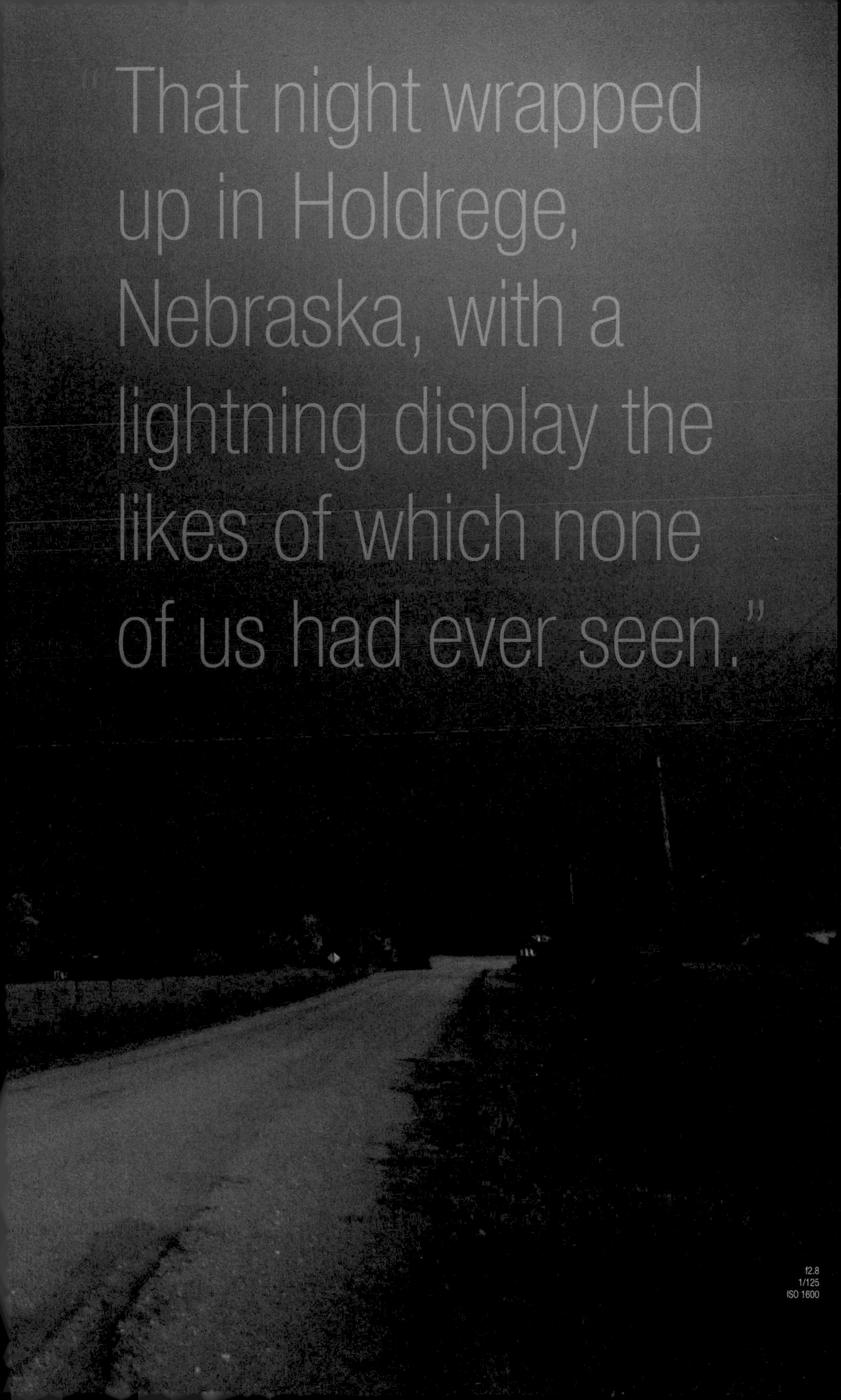

CHAPTER 8

NEBRASKA ALL OVER AGAIN

SOUTH DAKOTA
NEBRASKA
COLORADO

f2.8
1/125
ISO 1600

This storm intercept in extreme southwest Nebraska lasted for hours.

JUNE 16-17, 2011

SOUTH DAKOTA
NEBRASKA
COLORADO

◉ **REGINA** SK

● **SPEARFISHER** SD

● NORTH PLATTE NE

● STERLING CO

○ McCOOK NE

○ HOLDREGE NE

● GRAND ISLAND NE

● KEARNEY NE

◉ REGINA SK

By this time of the year—early summer for some, but well into the storm-chasing season—I have probably listened to every song on my **iPod**® a dozen times.

On deck was another long road trip from Saskatchewan to Nebraska. This time around the Tornado Truck would have two new riders, Nick Schenher and Ben Tucker.

We were headed south toward what was shaping up as a two-day Nebraska tornadofest. En route we spent a night in Spearfisher, South Dakota, getting to know each other along the way. It was shaping up to be a very difficult system to forecast, so we stayed up late and woke up early in order to examine the various weather models, trying to pinpoint a target for the following day.

One thing was for sure…all of the ingredients were in place for severe weather over Nebraska in the next couple of days.

Approaching our target area shortly after noon on June 19, 2011 it was becoming apparent that we were slightly out of position. Storms had begun to develop in Colorado and we would need to move west quickly if we were going to be properly positioned to catch a tornado.

CHASERCODE

Music

Here are my driving favorites—Helter Skelter, Walk This Way, Detroit Rock City, You Spin Me Round, Lunatic Fringe, Let's Get It Started, New Orleans Is Sinking.

The first night of the trip was spent in Spearfisher, SD. On the way south we stopped on several occasions to get photos of the amazing scenery. (below)

Storms brewing on the horizon in South Dakota. Too far to get to so we wait for the next one. (right)

f4
1/500
ISO 200

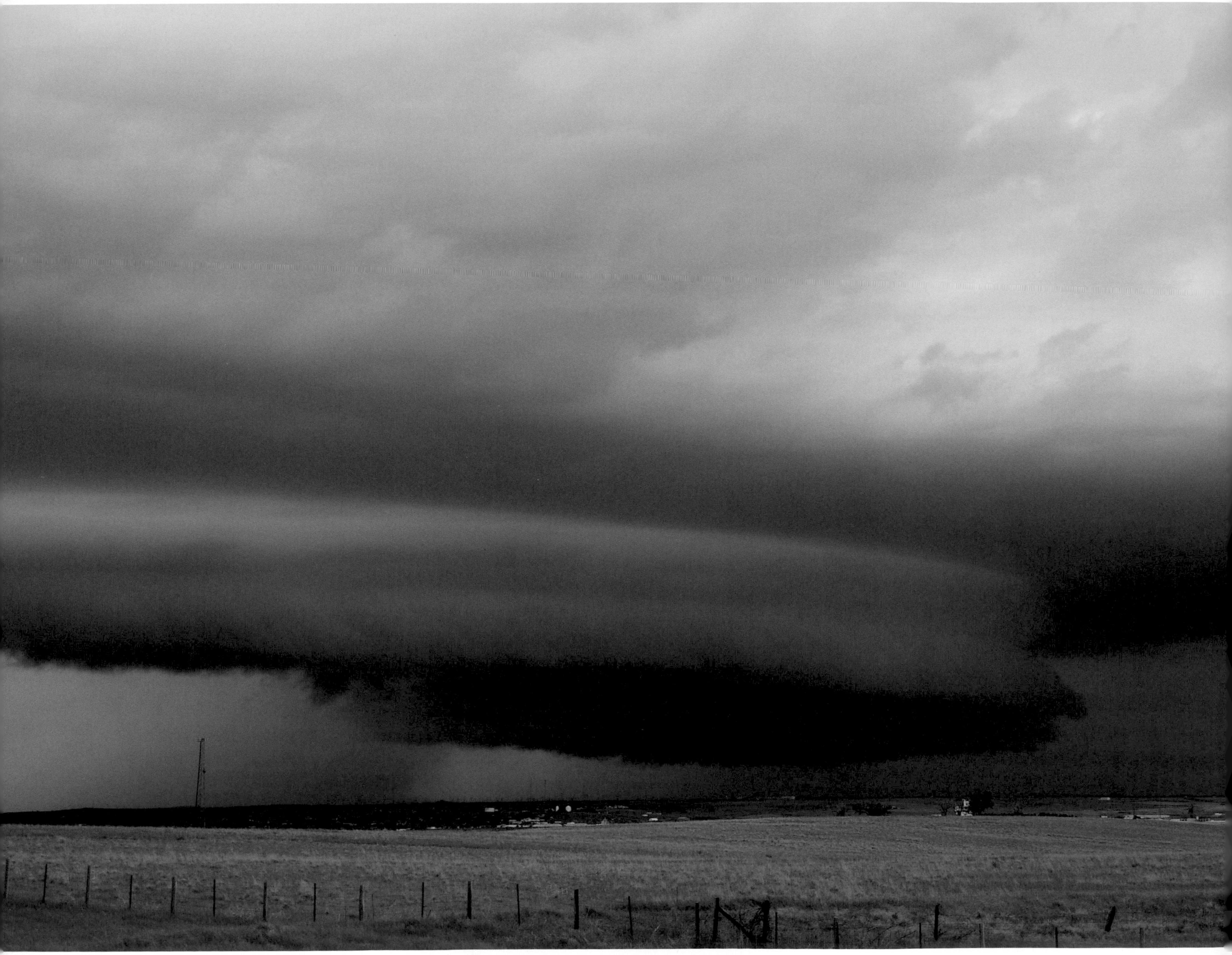

A supercell developed in western Nebraska. This was our first intercept of the day and the potential looked very good. (left)

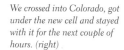

We crossed into Colorado, got under the new cell and stayed with it for the next couple of hours. (right)

There was great structure on this storm and each town in the path had the tornado sirens blaring. Several tornadoes were reported throughout the day as about a dozen really good storms moved through the state. (right)

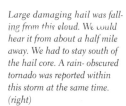

Large damaging hail was falling from this cloud. We could hear it from about a half mile away. We had to stay south of the hail core. A rain-obscured tornado was reported within this storm at the same time. (right)

f3.5
1/160
ISO 400

f2.8
1/40
ISO 2000

One of my chase partners, Nick Schenher, watches the approaching storm. I love that it looks like a caption bubble above his head. (top left)

We were not alone. Several local spotters and chasers were in the area watching the storm and reporting what they were seeing. (left)

CHASERCODE

Warning Polygon

In the United States, areas under severe weather warnings such as tornado warnings are shown on maps using polygons to show areas under the potential threat.

The Hook

On radar, the reflective radar can provide indication of tornado potential when the storm image has a pronounced hook on the tail end. This is a very good indicator that a storm is in fact producing a tornado. Chasers get very excited when they see the hook image on the radar screen.

We removed the screen and shot several hundred lightning photos from the comfort of the hotel room. The tornado warnings were sounding but the storm passed to the north of Holdrege. (above)

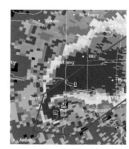

Traveling west on I-80 from North Platte, we encountered our first cell of the day just before we arrived at the Colorado border. This was an impressive storm that appeared to be rotating. As we approached, the tornado sirens went off and we hoped to get our first intercept of the trip.

We got up under the rotation and were hit with hail and heavy rain. We needed to make a decision quickly to stay with this storm or find another, because this one was headed into an area of the state with a very poor road network for chasing.

We opted to move on and catch the next storm as it developed in Colorado. This turned out to be a good decision but cost us about two hours of drive time before we were able to get back into position for a great storm that came complete with a tornado warning.

The next three hours brought rotating wall clouds, large hail, storm sirens and at least one large rain-wrapped tornado. That night wrapped up in Holdrege, Nebraska with a lightning display the likes of which none of us had ever seen. After watching the magnificent spectacle fade into the distance, we checked into the motel and settled in to edit photos and get a blog post together.

As we sat working, we heard a distant rumble of thunder. Checking the radar, we discovered that a new storm had developed and was taking direct aim at Holdrege. As we watched the storm progress from inside the hotel, the warning polygon on the radar popped up indicating that we were now in a tornado warned area. I ran to the front desk to find out if there was a safe room in the motel, advising the frightened clerk to pay attention to the warnings and be ready to inform the guests of pending danger.

CHASERCODE

Chaser Gear

What storm chasers have in their kit. Laptops, cell phones, first aid kit, cameras, video cameras, satellite antenna and receiver, iPod®, extra spare tire, power inverters, tripods, GPS, paper maps, weather band radio and helmets.

f3.2
1/1600
ISO 400

As we came over the hill, two tornadoes were on the ground, one to our left and one to our right. We caught the last few seconds of both. This is the only photo I snapped before they disappeared. (top-left)

The radar picture was showing the size and intensity of this storm. At one point we saw at least seven areas that had potential tornadoes. (top–right)

Our route was blocked by debris left behind by one of the many tornadoes reported on this day. (right)

f2.8
1/40
ISO 2000

f5.6
1.3sec
ISO 640

As we arrived in Holdrege, NE to spend the night, we were treated to another fantastic light show. Nebraska never disappoints. (left)

Moments later the tornado sirens went off; we could plainly see the storm heading directly for us, complete with constant cloud to ground lightning strikes. With one last check of the radar confirming we were in the line of fire, I rushed back to the front desk and told the clerk to contact all the rooms and to take cover.

Thankfully, the storm skirted just north of town and with that, the fireworks were finally done for the night.

The following day was a complete disaster: picked the wrong target, out of position, caught the tail end of two tornadoes, speeding ticket, lost time, storms gone, chase done…

It was a long drive back to Saskatchewan.

"When a giant supercell with 80 mph winds, possible tornadoes, lightning and hail is bearing down on you, it's a really unnerving feeling."

CHAPTER 9
NORTH OF THE BORDER

SASKATCHEWAN

f4.5
1/100
ISO 320

*I was out chasing a small
thunderstorm near Assiniboia,
Saskatchewan with my good*

SASKATCHEWAN

◉ **REGINA** SK

● **CORONACH** SK

○ INDIAN HEAD SK

○ PENSE SK

○ DOG RIVER SK
(ROULEAU SK)

● ESTEVAN SK

○ ASSINIBOIA SK

○ DUNDURN SK

○ MANKOTA SK

● WEYBURN SK

◉ REGINA SK

JUNE 29 - JULY 29, 2011

The month of June was drawing to a close and storm chasing in the United States for the 2011 season was done. I would be chasing north of the border, on the Canadian Prairies.

Generally speaking, the intensity of severe weather and the potential for devastating tornadoes diminishes as the season progresses and moves further north. I say "generally" because there have been notable exceptions to this rule in recent years. In 2007, we saw two significant tornadoes roar through southern Manitoba: one at the town of Elie and the other at Pipestone.

The Elie storm was an F5 rated tornado, ranking it as the strongest winds ever seen in Canada.

The 2011 Canadian chase season represented a new beginning in my storm chasing career.

I was live-Tweeting storm warnings and severe weather reports while live-streaming chases on my website, TornadoHunter.com. This signaled a new and significant media component to every chase I was on: I enjoyed the pleasure of introducing a whole new group of people to the world of storm chasing. On top of all that, I snapped my favorite images of the year on the Canadian side of the border and witnessed some of the most intense and beautiful storms of my career.

That was the good news. The bad news, for me anyway, was that tornadoes were an extremely rare phenomenon on the Canadian Prairies in 2011. In fact, I did not witness any tornadoes on the Canadian side of the border in 2011. The year's only real significant tornado event in Canada happened at Goderich, Ontario, about 2,500 miles away from our chase position.

CHASERCODE

Elie by Numbers
F5, 40 kilometers (25 mi) west of Winnipeg, June 22, 2007. 0 injuries, 0 deaths, 6:30 PM, traveled about 3.7 mi, 330 yd wide, 40 minute lifespan.

2007/06/22

This photo of the Elie, Manitoba F5 tornado shows the early stage of its life cycle. Photographed by Jeannine Guyot from about 4 1/2 miles away. (above)

Talk about timing. I was shooting to get the lightning strikes in the distance. On this shot I got them but I also had a very close strike behind me during the same exposure. This is the light source that is illuminating the foreground and the truck. Notice the reflection on the truck; you can see the strike behind the camera position. (right)

This storm near Griffin, SK originated in the Big Muddy Badlands region of Saskatchewan in July, 2011. Andrea Clarke is the photographer and I am so proud to include this image, as Andrea is a former photo workshop client. (right)

f5
2sec
ISO 320

An incredible lightning strike near Coronach, SK. I was chasing with Preston Kanak and he caught all of this on video. Spectacular night.

One area of Saskatchewan that was on the receiving end of a fairly regular stream of storms flowing up from Montana was the Big Muddy Badlands region, including Coronach, Big Beaver and Rockglen. Numerous storms raged across the area throughout the season; it seemed that every time I found myself out chasing, I was driving through this region.

The storm at Pense, SK heads east towards the capital city of Regina, SK. (above)

Southern Saskatchewan experienced once in a generation flooding in the spring and summer of 2011. This shot taken north of Estevan, SK. (right)

Southern Saskatchewan proved to be the most fertile ground for the majority of our chase opportunities. The Saskatchewan season started in a big way, with epic and historic flooding in the southeast sector of the province–the same flooding that devastated Minot and other areas of North Dakota.

Property damage from the flooding and record-breaking insurance claims for hail across Saskatchewan made 2011 a season that will not be forgotten. In fact, *The Weather Network* ranked the story of severe weather in Saskatchewan as the Canadian weather event of the year.

In the absence of tornadoes, lightning became the preferred subject for photography, while the towns and villages of the southern plains became the canvas. Pense, Coronach, Weyburn, Mankota, Assiniboia (all in Saskatchewan) and many others played host to our chasing team as we criss-crossed the province in July and August.

The closest call of the year. This lightning strike was the one that ended my day.

My favorite image of the year was also one of my closest brushes with a lightning strike–a little too close for comfort. It happened at Pense, Saskatchewan on July 3, 2011, generated by the same storm system that was responsible for millions of dollars of damage in the Regina area.

This storm wreaked havoc on the Saskatchewan Roughrider's CFL football game being played at Mosaic stadium. Golf-ball sized hail tore a swath through the city, causing extensive damage and prompting a tornado warning.

CHASERCODE

Hail Facts

Chasers refer to hail in the following sizes - pea, dime, nickel, quarter, golf ball, orange, baseball, grapefruit and bowling ball. Golf-ball or larger is considered damaging.

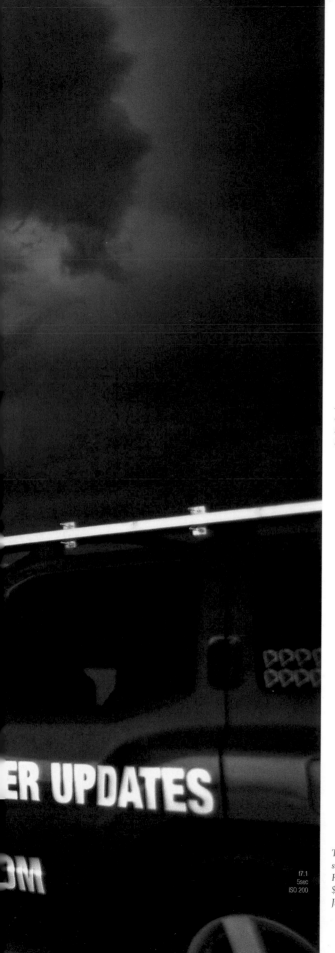

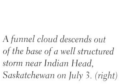

The stop we made at Pense was truly one of the best decisions of the season. With me on this chase were Vanessa Neufeld, Notanee Bourassa and Preston Kanak. (left)

A funnel cloud descends out of the base of a well structured storm near Indian Head, Saskatchewan on July 3. (right)

f2.8
1/2500
ISO 320

This storm dropped golf-ball sized hail on the city of Regina, causing a reported $1 million in damage claims. July 3, 2011. (right)

f7.1
5sec
ISO 200

f7.1
1/3200
ISO 500

On July 27, 2011, Notanee
Bourassa and I chased south
of Moose Jaw, cross country
to the east toward Regina
and eventually all the way
to Melville, SK. (right)

f2.8
1/1250
ISO 250

The month of July produced
wave after wave of thunderstorms
in southern Saskatchewan.
This one is just north of Moose
Jaw, SK on July 8, 2011. (left)

Rouleau, SK, AKA Dog River,
saw an intense rotating storm
roll though on July 27, 2011.
(right)

f6.3
1sec
ISO 400

A dangerous storm system
rolled past Saskatoon on July
12, 2011. Nick Schenher and
I caught up to this 'mother-
ship' at Dundurn, SK. (left)

f4
1/250
ISO 200

f4,5
1/200
ISO 250

DOG RIVER

Another incredible chase ended near the North Dakota border at Estevan, Saskatchewan where I witnessed an amazing light show generated by what might have been the most perfectly structured supercell I have ever witnessed, framed by a moonless canopy of stars.

I sat on the hood of my truck just watching that storm disappear into the distance for about two hours before starting the long drive home.

A great night of storm chasing near the US border with Saskatchewan. These two shots were taken west of Estevan, SK.

f2.8
13sec
ISO 1600

I installed a hail guard to protect the windshield from hail and debris. This image was shot east of Assiniboia in mid July. (left)

I passed through Assiniboia, SK several time this chase season. (left)

f4
10sec
ISO 320

The elevators at Woodrow, SK provide the perfect framework for this lightning shot.

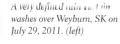

The end is near! The sky turned to fire in Weyburn, SK on July 29, 2011. The ragged wall cloud descending from the base of the storm foreshadowed what could happen if a tornado was to hit the small city. (right)

A very defined rain and air washes over Weyburn, SK on July 29, 2011. (left)

As the sun dropped to the horizon the wall cloud that had prompted the tornado warning for Weyburn, SK, glowed orange, as if on fire. (left)

Storms rolled non-stop through July. The province saw at least 20 days of severe weather that culminated with an intense system that passed through the province on July 29, 2011, complete with reports of extreme wind speeds in excess of 70 mph, and straight-line wind damage.

My chase that day began in Weyburn, which is where the tornado warnings began. It was there I snapped an image that I dubbed the 'Wall Cloud Of Fire.' *(above and right)*

As the system hit Weyburn and the warnings were issued, a pronounced wall cloud descended out of the base of the rotating storm above the city. In-flow winds indicated that this beast was gaining strength and the structure of the storm was perfect.

CHASERCODE

In-Flow Wind

Is air in the boundary layer (close to the ground) being ingested into the updraft portion of the storm. If you are looking at the storm and the wind is at your back, you are experiencing in-flow winds.

CHAPTER 9
NORTH OF
THE BORDER

At least one tornado was reported in the Griffin area east of Weyburn. High winds caused significant damage in a region already reeling from the worst flooding in more than a generation.

The storms continued to back-build in a line to the northwest; eventually a damaging cell brought the high winds slamming through the capital region causing widespread damage in the city of Regina. At one point this storm was travelling at a ground speed of over 60 mph.

Whenever straight-line winds cause this level of damage, citizen tornado reports always pour in, but it soon became clear that the winds from this storm were the culprit–the result of down-burst activity, not the updraft activity a tornado would cause.

Storm chasing in July in Saskatchewan was busy, beautiful and went out just as it arrived: with a bang.

CHASERCODE

Storm Speed

The ground speed of the storms plays a huge role in how to chase and at times even if we chase. Generally storm motions are between 15-30 mph. This is very chase-able. Sometimes however, storm speeds are in excess of 50-60 mph and this is not only more dangerous but depending on the location can be almost impossible to chase safely.

The rain and hail core passed over the city of Weyburn and the area of rotation passed just south of town. (top)

I used a relatively slow shutter speed of a half second and mounted the camera on a tripod. Winds of over 70 mph accompanied this and other storm cells in the area, doing considerable damage. (bottom)

I sat under the Weyburn storm for about a half hour as it passed by. The rain-free base of the storm produced several lowerings but no tornadoes. (right)

f3.2
15sec
ISO 500

From Weyburn, I blasted west
to try and intercept a storm
moving in from the Swift
Current area. I intercepted
near Drinkwater, SK, however
at that time the storm was
moving at 65 mph. It contin-
ued on without me, doing
significant wind damage
in the city of Regina. (left)

I stopped in Drinkwater, SK to get some lightning shots as the storm roared past. Despite the strong winds I was able to get a few cool shots. (below)

"We punched through the hail and rain and came out on the other side perfectly positioned for any tornadoes."

f4.5
1/100
ISO 640

CHAPTER 10
REVISITING PIPESTON

SASKATCHEWAN
MANITOBA

*As Nick and I arrive in the
Pipestone, Manitoba region
the storm seems to take
on a more ominous feel.*

CHAPTER 10
**REVISTING
PIPESTONE**

SASKATCHEWAN
MANITOBA

 REGINA SK

MOOSOMIN SK

ELKHORN MB

CROMER MB

PIPESTONE MB

DELORAINE MB

REGINA SK

f4.5
1/100
ISO 640

f4
1/125
ISO 400

f3.5
1/100
ISO 640

f4.5
1/100
ISO 640

The rain-free area of the storm was distinct and we managed to stay out of any rain and hail for most of the evening. (right)

The Regina Exhibition was in full swing. The midway was hopping and more than 70,000 people came through the turnstiles hoping to enjoy themselves on the rides, play some games, watch a concert and taste the food.

As we passed through Cromer, MB a tornado warning was issued by Environment Canada. (left)

CHASERCODE

Environment Canada

Is the equivalent to the National Weather Service in the United States. EC issues Severe Storm Warnings, Tornado Watches and Tornado Warnings throughout Canada.

I used my windshield mounted phone as a video camera to stream our chasing live on my website. (bottom left)

As the evening wore on the storm actually seemed to slow down. On several occasions we were able to stop and shoot for several minutes before needing to reposition. (bottom right)

Far from their minds was the potential for severe weather to interrupt the fun and shut down the show. But for me, that was a very distinct possibility. I had been hired to keep an eye to the sky and report on severe weather risks. My role was to help the emergency management team make informed decisions about severe weather and keep the crowds safe.

On August 6, 2011, a series of storms developed above the city of Regina and we had to shut down the rides temporarily. This happened on several occasions throughout the day but the worst of the storms passed without incident.

The next morning at the management briefing I informed the team that this day was significantly high risk and I was worried about crowd safety. It was clear that we would see the kind of storms that produce tornadoes and even **Environment Canada** issued an early tornado watch for most of Southern Saskatchewan and Western Manitoba.

As the afternoon began, two significant storms cells did develop but fortunately for the crowd the storms began east of Regina and continued east toward Manitoba. With the risk for the Exhibition over, I packed the truck and headed out after the growing storms with Nick Schenher.

Despite the name 'storm chaser' the best way to 'chase' a storm is to intercept it or cut it off. By moving toward a storm that is moving toward you the time to get into position is reduced and you have a better chance of getting great photos and video. On this chase, however, we did not have the luxury of letting the storm come to us, we had to chase it from behind. Even though we had a great visual it took almost three hours before we were able to catch up to this now towering cumulonimbus cloud. We punched through the hail and rain and came out on the other side perfectly positioned for any tornadoes.

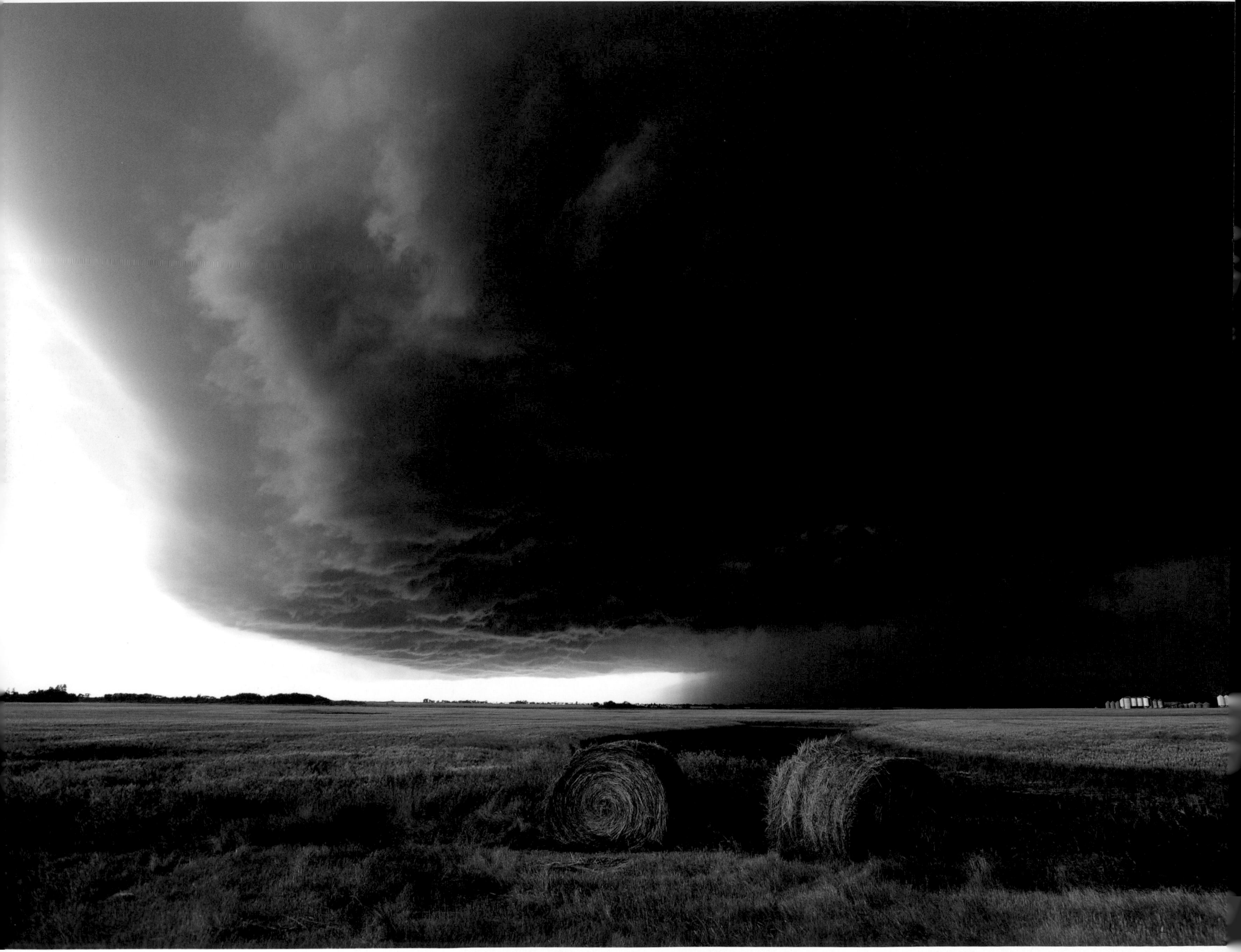

f4.5
1/400
ISO 640

At this point we had pushed the truck through the hail core to get to the target location. Fortunately the hail was no bigger than nickles. (right)

f4.5
1/400
ISO 640

Nick and I moved location several times but it seemed like there was always something to shoot. This image was shot from the moving truck. (left)

CHASERCODE

Photo Crazy

While chasing I will shoot anywhere from a few hundred to a few thousand photos every day depending on the weather conditions. The worse the weather, the better.

Repositioning continued over the next couple of hours as the storm continued to grow and change. The tornado warning was issued and we were in perfect position. I took **thousands of photographs** and as we reached a crossroad in the southwest corner of the province of Manitoba, I realized we were at Pipestone. This was the site of the dramatic 2007 F4 twister that was seen around the world on YouTube™ and on *The Discovery Channel*. It was apparent that this storm was exhibiting many of the same characteristics and appeared likely to produce a large damaging wedge tornado.

Nick and I spent a lot of time under this storm and we collected some great footage. After dark the show continued as we captured some significant lightning strikes and then made our way home to Regina.

f4.5
1/250
ISO 640

Another shot taken while the truck is moving. At this point we just didn't have time to stop, the storm would have overtaken us.

A slow shutter speed allows me to capture the effects of the strong winds on the grass and trees. This image was taken near Pipestone, MB.

After dark the light show continued throughout western Manitoba. It was a late night but well worth the trip.

" Two cells were converging and the sun provided the pallette that was painting the cloud base. We shot for over an hour until the light began to fade and the rain closed in. "

CHAPTER 11
THE HOME STRETCH

SASKATCHEWAN

◉ **REGINA** SK

○ **SOUTHEY** SK

○ CORONACH SK

○ AVONLEA SK

○ OUTLOOK SK

● MELVILLE SK

◉ REGINA SK

f2.8
6sec
ISO 1600

AUGUST, 2011

August is the month known as the dog days of summer for storm chasers. The really serious storms are done, the atmospheric energy has diminished, snow is still a long way away and we won't see good Northern Lights for a couple of months. At least that's the theory.

This year was a bit different and the photographic results tell the story of a truly remarkable August weather-wise in Canada.

Perhaps the most breathtaking 'storm' of the year took place on August 5, 2011, when an intense solar storm struck the earth, creating a spectacular display of aurora that turned the moonless sky into a canopy of color and dancing shapes. This was followed closely by the Perseid meteor shower and then a series of days that produced beautiful storms in southern Saskatchewan. The most picturesque of the month was the supercell that descended on the Coronach/Rockglen Saskatchewan region at sunset on August 14.

The Qu'Appelle Valley in southern Saskatchewan was lit up by this storm level aurora. I was accompanied on my favorite chase of the season by my good friend Angie. (above)

The Northern Lights were at storm level in early August. This gorgeous farm seemed the perfect fit to include in the shot. (right)

CHASERCODE

Aurora Photography

When shooting aurora I typically have a high ISO such as 1600, a wide aperture like 2.8 and I try to keep my shutter speeds no longer than six seconds. Any longer and you tend to lose the streakiness of the light.

f2.8
6sec
ISO 1600

I was out on August 13 with a large group of students from my photo workshop giving a lesson on night shooting. I caught a Perseid during one of my test shots! (right)

While the Saskatchewan Legislature stands proudly on the banks of Wascana Lake in Regina, a Perseid meteor penetrates the atmosphere leaving a gorgeous tail. (left)

This image taken after midnight on August 12 is illuminated by an almost full moon. The long exposure reveals the canopy of stars as well as making the foreground look like daylight. (left)

f2.8
13sec
ISO 400

CHAPTER 11
THE HOME STRETCH

David Sampson and I headed out to intercept storms moving into Saskatchewan from Montana on August 14. This image was taken near Coronach, SK.

f2.8
1/50
ISO 400

Another shot from Coronach. The clouds this evening made so many unique and memorable formations. It was quiet and calm but the lightning was flashing all around us.

The last shot of the night was a doozy! This image is cropped from a much larger, very overexposed image. My settings were correct for a much smaller lightning strike but then the mother of all strikes hit causing the overexposure.

As darkness fell, David and I stopped one last time to get some lightning shots.

My good friend David Sampson was on board for this trip and we experienced one of the major pitfalls of chasing. After several hours of driving, we reached our destination and started shooting as the scene unfolding in front of us was brilliant but likely fleeting. Lightning was striking at close range in every direction around us. Two cells were converging and the sun provided the palette that was painting the cloud base. We shot for over an hour until the light began to fade and the rain closed in. We then followed the storm shooting more lightning, hoping to catch the best lightning strike of the season. We were literally in the middle of nowhere, or at least we could see it from where we were. Even the folks who live there will tell you so. That's when we realized that the truck was dangerously low on fuel.

We called ahead to Coronach, then to Willow Bunch, the closest towns. No gas stations open at this hour. We called to Assiniboia which was a long drive away and we weren't sure we could even make it that far. They were open but not for much longer. We raced away from our lightning producing storm and made it to the gas pump on fumes.

I love the camaraderie involved in chasing, however, when it comes to photographing storms sometimes all those people get in the way. There is significantly less chaser traffic on the Canadian prairies. (left)

Then the Canadian tornado story of the year happened at beautiful and historic Goderich, Ontario, on the shores of Lake Huron. A line of tornado-warned storms crossed the lake from Michigan and made a direct hit on the resort town causing extensive damage to the downtown which was described as resembling a war zone. Goderich is about two hours west of Toronto and this disaster brought home for many the fears so familiar to residents of the plains and southern United States. One man was killed in the Ontario storm that caused millions of dollars in damage.

One aspect of this tragedy that has affected me personally this year is the lack of preparedness in Canada for such events. I was amazed while I was in Joplin that based on the scale of destruction a relatively small number of people perished. The low body count was in my opinion due to the nature of the warnings and preparedness provided to the people of Joplin. Residents told me that they had upwards of 17 minutes warning that a large devastating tornado was headed their way. As terrifying as that storm was, 17 minutes is incredible. Many residents received text message warnings from the National Weather Service; broadcast media raised the alarm on radio and television interrupting programming to issue the dire warnings, and as the storm approached the tornado sirens wailed through town 17 minutes before it struck. Joplin could have been much worse and my fear is that if a tornado on the scale of Pipestone or Elie, Manitoba would hit an urban area in Canada as it did in Joplin the death toll would be much higher. None of the warning mechanisms that exist in the United States exist in Canada.

This early August storm creates a beautiful contrast against the stereotypical prairie image of a ripened wheat field. (top)

Goderich, Ontario was the site of an F3 rated tornado. This scary image shows in detail that the dangerous part of a tornado is not how the wind blows, but rather what the wind blows. Photo by Mark Robinson (bottom)

A spider web of lightning frames the Saskatchewan Legislature in Regina, SK.

f16
1/8
ISO 200

Lake Diefenbaker in central Saskatchewan. A late summer storm rumbles over the lake. I was on a camping trip with my family. Figures we would get a storm! (left)

The boat launch at Douglas Provincial Park on Lake Diefenbaker. (above)

I looked at the models and watched the forecast closely. The next few days were going to be hot and sunny with little or no chance of storms. My kids and I packed up the trailer and headed out camping as I tried to salvage a bit of R&R before the warm weather left. I brought my camera of course and it was a good thing, because on the third day camping a small storm system moved through the central Saskatchewan region where we were staying. Although the storm had no potential for producing tornadoes it did produce some excellent lightning.

My favorite lightning shots are those taken during daylight hours or during twilight. I find that the combination of lightning and being able to see the terrain and structures and the depth of the clouds is so much more interesting than lightning against a dark sky.

There are some challenges, however. When shooting lightning during daylight hours the shutter speed becomes a real issue; too long and the photo is overexposed, too fast and you cannot capture the lightning strike. In camera terms, lightning is a fairly long event.

It seems fast and over in the blink of an eye but the camera doesn't see it that way. The camera can fire off four or five photos during one lightning strike. Playing with the settings and understanding how to get the results took a lot of practice and a lot of trial and error. Generally, my daytime lightning shots will have a very low ISO such as 100 and an aperture setting suitable to expose the lightning properly, such as F11. Then I will adjust my shutter speed until the exposure on the overall image looks good. And then I shoot lots on continuous shutter. On some lightning shoots I will burn through 1500+ images. The trick is not to get impatient.

Another challenge when shooting lightning is safety. I have probably been very lucky to this point but I also take some precautions to stay safe. When possible, I mount the camera on a tripod and trigger the camera remotely from inside my truck. When it is raining, I will mount the tripod in the back of the truck and open the rear hatch so I don't need to get out. And most importantly, I try not to put myself into harm's way. I know when the strikes are getting too close for comfort…and I move.

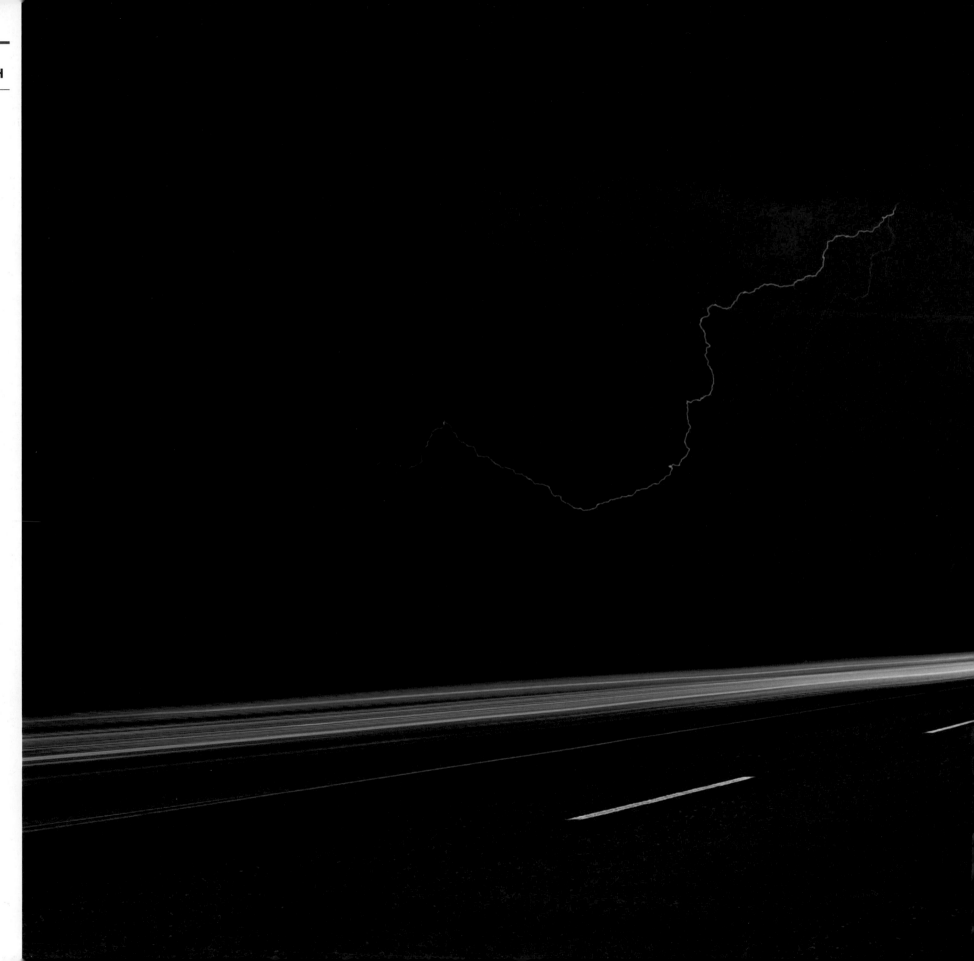

CHAPTER 11
THE HOME STRETCH

SASKATCHEWAN

REGINA SK

SOUTHEY SK

CORONACH SK

AVONLEA SK

OUTLOOK SK

MELVILLE SK

REGINA SK

The lake was actually fairly choppy, however the long shutter speed of 30 seconds was enough to even out the look of the water. Note the 'foggy' look around the rocks. This is a result of many waves hitting the rocks during the exposure. (page 151-152)

I love car trails, lightning, stars and storms as subjects. This image combines two of them. The car passed my location as the lightning was sparking up in front of us. Lovely cloud-to-ground lightning, the most dangerous kind. I love it. (previous page)

The last epic lightning strike. Fitting that it happened in Saskatchewan near the city of Melville. This was very near the site of my first ever prairie storm close encounter, the one that got all of this started. (right)

The last chase of the year was on August 29, 2011 in Eastern Saskatchewan. Along with my chase partners Notanee and Martin, we worked our way east from Regina toward Melville. This was a low probability, late season chase but as darkness closed in, we found ourselves trapped between two intense storms that were producing some amazing lightning strikes. A grain terminal appeared to our east so we quickly parked the truck on a muddy grid road and set up the camera for a last ditch effort to catch lightning on the plains. I snapped off a relatively low number of images and on the 32nd frame as the rain began to beat against us–*crack!*–a dramatic double-forked cloud-to-ground strike at close range. I stopped the camera and checked the image on the screen. It was perfectly exposed and perfectly composed.

That's the way it goes when you are chasing storms. More than once this season, I found myself in perfect position under a perfect storm. Sometimes they produce dramatic results like a tornado or an amazing lightning strike and sometimes they die. It's like the last two minutes of a close football game. Sometimes they make the on-side kick, recover the ball and drive the length of the field for the game winning touchdown…and sometimes they take a knee and run out the clock.

f10
2.5 sec
ISO 320

f2.8
2.5sec
ISO 400

The city of Saskatoon and the South Saskatchewan River played host to the Aurora Borealis in September. The city lights dulled the action somewhat but it was still a great way to end the chase season.

Other Indie Ink books you might enjoy

Birth of a Boom: Lives & Legacies of Saskatchewan Entrepreneurs (2nd edition)
By Suzanne Paschall

Softcover $34.95
ISBN 978-0-9866936-4-9

The first book in the Birth of a Boom series, Lives & Legacies is a lavishly-illustrated personal account of 13 fascinating Saskatchewan entrepreneurs' roads to success and their contributions to the province's emerging great prosperity.

Birth of a Boom: Saskatchewan's Dawning Golden Age
By David Breen Seymour

Hardcover $39.95
ISBN 978-0-9866936-8-7

In this concise and well-researched second book in the Birth of a Boom Series, Seymour seeks out the most vibrant and successful societies in history: Ancient Athens, the Islamic Golden Age, and Enlightenment Scotland, then modernizes their lessons for modern-day Saskatchewan, which stands, he believes, on the cusp of its own Golden Age.

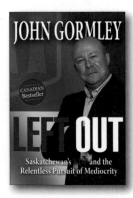

Left Out: Saskatchewan's NDP & the Relentless Pursuit of Mediocrity
By John Gormley

Softcover $19.95
ISBN 978-0-9866936-0-1

Edgy and thought-provoking, Left Out takes aim at the NDP, Saskatchewan's natural governing party since the 1940s. Outspoken broadcaster and writer John Gormley pulls no punches in an entertaining and informative account of Saskatchewan politics that is both a lament and a challenge he issues to a new generation of voters.

To learn where to purchase these books, or to find out more about Indie Ink, visit us at indieinkpublishing.com.
And don't forget to like us on Facebook.